The

# of Justice

ROBERT F. KENNEDY

Edited by Theodore J. Lowi

The lines on page 106 are from "Mending Wall" from *Complete Poems of Robert Frost.* Copyright 1930, 1939 by Holt, Rinehart and Winston, Inc. Copyright renewed © 1958 by Robert Frost. Reprinted by permission of Holt, Rinehart and Winston, Inc.

Chapter 4 is an expansion of "Robert Kennedy Defines the Menace," by Robert F. Kennedy, and appeared in *The New York Times Magazine* of October 13, 1963. © 1963 by The New York Times Company. Reprinted by permission.

The Pursuit of Justice
Robert F. Kennedy
edited by Theodore J. Lowi

Copyright 1964 by Robert F. Kennedy

This Reprinting in May, 2017 by Ishi Press in New York and Tokyo

with a new introduction by Sam Sloan
Copyright © 2017 by Sam Sloan

ISBN 4-87187-783-3
978-4-87187-783-1

Ishi Press International
1664 Davidson Avenue, Suite 1B
Bronx NY 10453-7877
USA
1-917-659-3397
1-917-507-7226
samhsloan@gmail.com

Printed in the United States of America

The Pursuit of Justice
by Robert F. Kennedy
edited by Theodore J. Lowi

Introduction by Sam Sloan

These essays by Robert F. Kennedy, grew out of speeches, travel and his experience as Attorney General and a United States Senator. This book was published in 1964 while he was alive, unlike other books that were not published until after his death.

The office of Attorney General is in many respects the hot corner of political combat. All of the "hard cases" of law enforcement, public administration and governmental services eventually find their way to his desk. It is impossible, therefore, for an Attorney General not to have taken a position on most of the basic issues of his day. And it is impossible to conceive of a time when all parties interested in the stakes of government could be pleased with a decision, or a non-decision-of the man who holds the office.

As a consequence, few posts in government share such public attention as that of the Attorney General. When the holder of the office is also a member of the innermost governing circle, public attention turns to fascination. Such a situation must be blood-curdling for the incumbent because the fascination is not of the passive and pleasant sort of engagement associated with the best television programs. The Attorney General is taken every way but lightly.

This volume contains twelve essays or "position papers" dealing with those problems with which one such Attorney General was most occupied and preoccupied during his issue-laden three years and nine months of service. During that time the United States faced many major crises at home and abroad and, for better or worse, met them. In meeting them, the Administration broke many precedents and established a few others. In so doing it gave the American people a political orientation stronger than any witnessed since the Roosevelt One Hundred Days. These essays treat many of those issues with considerable depth and clarity of argument and opinion Characteristically, it is not possible to take this book lightly, whether the subject is wiretapping, the radical right, Berlin. price-fixing, counterinsurgency, the injustices of poverty, or the dereliction of the lawyer's duties in effecting compliance of civil rights statutes. But within the wide range of subject and opinions, formal and informal there is an unmistakable unity. Professor Lowi describes it in his Editor's Foreword: "In all of this there is a characteristic answer that has, perhaps, come to be taken as a Kennedy family trait. This is the confounded optimism that individual will and action can in fact set the world to rights." The volume opens with a special chapter written by Robert F. Kennedy as a review of his years of public service and a statement of personal beliefs.

The closing sentences of THE PURSUIT OF JUSTICE: ... however wise our efforts may be in unconventional diplomacy and unconventional warfare, however sensible our diversity of weapons and strategy, however great our military power and determined our counteroffensive of ideas, there is yet another obstacle to our opening to the future. That is the image of the future we project by our own example. What substance can we provide for the international hopes we can kindle? "Thus we end where we began. We must get our own house in order. We must because it is right. We must because it is might."

Robert F. Kennedy was born on November 20, 1925. He is often regard as a weak second brother to John F. Kennedy but in reality he was far better educated. He graduated from law school and passed the bar exam. John F. Kennedy did neither. He also wrote five books. There are lingering doubts as to if John F. Kennedy wrote his books, or did ghost writers hired by his father write them, as his father was grooming him to run for President.

Robert F. Kennedy was assassinated on June 6, 1968. Nobody knows why he was assassinated as the man who did it, Sirhan Sirhan, says he does not know why he did it either. It is fairly certain that had not Robert Kennedy been assassinated just minutes after winning the California primary, he would have been elected president of the United States and all of history from then until now would have been different. Would he have gotten us out of Vietnam, something Lyndon Johnson seemed unable to do?

He served as the United States junior senator from New York from January 1965 until his assassination in June 1968. He was previously the 64th US Attorney General from January 1961 to September 1964, serving under his older brother President John F. Kennedy and his successor, President Lyndon B. Johnson.

Now the largest bridge within New York City, the Tri-Borough Bridge, which is a combination of three bridges that connect Manhattan, Queens and the Bronx, had been renamed the Robert F. Kennedy Bridge, or simply the RFK Bridge. I must say that I am opposed to this. Travelers from out of town risk getting lost because of this renaming of the bridge.

Nowadays, we are hyper-sensitive about classified material with one presidential candidate accusing the other candidate of mishandling classified material and a distinguished military general being forced out of office because his mistress may have seen classified material. Much information about the Cuban Missile Crisis and about the Bay of Pigs Invasion remain classified to this day. Even on my own website there are memos I got as a result of Freedom of Information Act requests that contain classified information about American pilots who were killed during the Bay of Pigs invasion where this information is not available anywhere else as far as I know.

THEODORE J. LOWI, the editor of this volume, was Assistant Professor of Government at Cornell University. Theodore J. Lowi was born on July 9, 1931 in Gadsden, Alabama. He was educated at Michigan State University and Yale. Professor Lowi was a frequent contributor to the scholarly press and an occasional contributor to popular journals of opinion. He is author of a prize-winning work on New York City, At the Pleasure of the Mayor: Patronage and Power in New York City, 1898-1958. He died on February 17, 2017 in Ithaca, New York at age 85. His obituary said, "Ted was the most important social scientist to teach at Cornell in the school's entire history."

Sam Sloan
Bronx New York
USA

May 24, 2017

To my mother and father
for what they gave to the past and to the present
and to my children for what they may give the future

"We have the power to make this
the best generation of mankind in the history
of the world or to make it the last."

—JOHN F. KENNEDY
*Address before the 18th General
Assembly of the United Nations
September 20, 1963*

Contents

Foreword

The Departments of the Federal Government are organized according to functions or subject-matter areas. Treasury handles revenue and fiscal matters. State is responsible for foreign affairs. Health, Education, and Welfare contains the functions which provide it its name. But, as usual, there is one complicating exception. This is the Department of Justice, which, according to the public administrator, is organized around "process" rather than function or subject matter.

The Department of Justice literally cuts across the work of all other Departments and agencies as well as that of Congress and the courts. It must see to the "faithful execution of the laws," as opposed to the administration of programs. In other words, it handles the "hard cases" that cannot be routinely administered by the functional Departments and agencies.

The presiding office, the Attorney General, holds a position of politics in the highest sense of that word: He must make hard choices. His decisions and advice to the President on prosecutions, appeals and investigations must necessarily hurt some as they help others. If the Attorney General is to be of any value to his President, he must have intelligence and opinions on virtually every subject within the broad scope of Federal power. For a man who is willing to play such a role, the burdens of office must be far greater than the satisfactions. That Robert F. Kennedy was willing is a fact granted, to be sure, by even his severest critics.

What I have done here is to develop his public statements into a series of twelve essays—"position papers" they might be called in government. Sometimes this meant combining materials drawn from several speeches or statements before Congressional committees. But at all times the ideas and positions are those of Mr. Kennedy. Mr. Kennedy has written a new first chapter for this volume.

There is, it seems to me, a central theme or preoccupation throughout the book, regardless of subject. This has to do with the role of the individual in search of his own dignity. What forces have had an impact upon him? More importantly, what impact has he had upon those forces?

In all of this there is a characteristic answer that has, perhaps, come to be taken as a Kennedy family trait. This is the confounded optimism that individual will and action can, in fact, set the world to rights. His arguments on world affairs (stressing guerrilla warfare and youth in revolution) are, in this respect, indistinguishable from those on juvenile delinquency and civil rights.

It is not necessary to agree with everything to be read in the pages to follow. The pleasant thing to discover is that there *are* positions to be discovered and disputed.

THEODORE J. LOWI

Ithaca, New York

Part I

A PERSONAL REVIEW, A PERSONAL CREDO

"It is the essence of responsibility to put the public good ahead of personal gain. This still leaves room for individual goals and for the pursuit of them with energy and intelligence. This of course applies to daily life—to the family—as it does to politics."

CHAPTER 1

I Remember, I Believe

As far back as I can remember, politics was taken with special fervor and relish in our house. We came by it naturally on both sides of our family. Our Grandfather Fitzgerald—"Honey Fitz"—who had been a Congressman and Mayor of Boston, talked frequently with us about his colorful career which epitomized the rise of the Irish politician. But it was more than that. I can hardly remember a mealtime when the conversation was not dominated by what Franklin D. Roosevelt was doing or what was happening around the world.

Aside from my grandfather's stories, I suppose the election of 1936 is really my earliest recollection of politics and my family's intense interest in public affairs. But after that, events turned from interest into involvement for all of us. The depression was still with us and the government was just beginning to have an impact upon it. My father had served as the first chairman of the Securities and Exchange Commission and as chairman of the Maritime Commission. In 1938 he was appointed Ambassador to England and there we saw the approaching war and repeatedly heard discussions

3

about England's lack of preparedness for it.

We went to Germany. The sight then of Nazism and storm troopers will never allow any of us to forget the price of dissolution and tyranny. Our oldest brother, Joe, was in Spain during part of the Spanish Civil War and President Kennedy was in Poland just prior to the time Germany invaded, setting off the Second World War.

All of this contrasted, of course, with our experiences in the United States. We lived in the suburbs of New York City and attended school there until we went to England. We spent our summers on Cape Cod. But it was impossible for even a child of my years not to see the contrast between the good fortune of my family and the problems and difficulties which befell other families through no fault of their own. Our parents made certain that we did. And more than that, our father repeatedly impressed upon us that nowhere but in the United States could he have achieved what he did; that we owed our blessings to the American system of government and therefore had an obligation to participate in public life. But I don't think any of us thought of public service as a sacrifice or as a means strictly of repaying a beneficent country. We looked to it as an opportunity for an exciting and fulfilling way of life. Since public affairs had dominated so much of our actions and discussions, public life seemed really an extension of family life.

Joe, had he lived, would surely have gone into politics, and in that event President Kennedy more than likely would have concentrated on writing. When I finished law school, I considered public life as one of several possible careers. At one time I thought seriously of practicing law in a private firm. But nothing seemed to hold the promise of a true career—the chance for responsibility at a young age or the opportunity for achievement—as did working for the government. I

4

participated in all of President Kennedy's campaigns for the House of Representatives and the Senate, worked as an assistant United States attorney in Brooklyn, served on the Hoover Commission and worked for Congressional committees.

By the time I became chief counsel of the Senate Rackets Investigating Committee in 1957, I knew that I would want to work for the government as long as I was able. Jimmy Hoffa provided a principal reason, for through him I discovered for myself the consequences of irresponsible use of power, how it threatened the freedom of all of us and what was required of each of us to stand against it.

The individual man, in whose hands democracy must put its faith and its fate, is capable of great heights of achievement. He also is capable of infinite degradation. Fortunately most of our institutions have safeguards which ultimately unseat a man when power results in arrogance and corruption. But often before justice is done the very institutions and values by which we attempt to order our lives can be undermined. This is especially true in our concentrated urban society and this was especially true of Mr. Hoffa.

Teamster Union control of transportation gives it a key position in the labor movement and great economic power. When there is corruption at the top and a close association with the underworld, as the investigations of the Senate Rackets Committee clearly disclosed, this kind of power is a threat to every decent person as well as to the very foundations of our democracy.

The committee's investigations had shown that while the vast majority of Teamsters were honest, hard-working men, power had corrupted some of their leaders. Worse yet, the corruption was spreading. Armed with great power and a vast treasury and guided by a philosophy that every man has his

5

price, Mr. Hoffa and his henchmen used intimidation and violence and, finally, a desperate, massive assault on the jury system to retain their hold on the union. Finally, this year Mr. Hoffa and six associates were convicted of jury tampering in four different trials. Later, a jury which included eight union members found Mr. Hoffa guilty of defrauding the Teamsters Union pension fund of more than $20 million—a cynical betrayal of the trust of working men and women.

Mr. Hoffa even corrupted one of his lawyers, a respected member of the Nashville, Tennessee, bar, who was convicted of jury tampering and disbarred. During 1961-64, juries in federal courts convicted 110 Teamster Union officials and associates of Mr. Hoffa of crimes involving misuse of union funds and abuse of union power.

The case heightens the awareness of the dangers of power without purpose, of power sought and used merely for the sake of power, of power as pure self-indulgence. But one can go too far in reaction and conclude that all power is evil and that no human can be so entrusted. If we really believed this, we would have to abandon social life altogether.

The real problem of power, of the concentration of power, is not its existence, because we cannot wish it away. The problem of power is how to achieve its responsible use rather than its irresponsible and indulgent use—of how to get men of power to live *for* the public rather than *off* the public. Defined this way, there are two approaches to the problem and these must be employed simultaneously. They are not novel with me. They are built into the American system, but occasionally are forgotten or misunderstood.

First, it is necessary to mistrust personal power enough to provide for some restraints upon its use. This is the idea of political competition that underlies everything else in the

American political system and the Constitution. Do not deprive a man of his capacity to act. Just be sure that he in turn is willing to obey the rules. Nobody ever enunciated the rule of competition as well as James Madison, justly credited as the Father of the Constitution. To Madison, the solution of the problem of power could be found in the natural diversity of faculties and interests among men. If these were allowed to flourish, no one set of interests and no one person could go too far in pursuit of a goal without bringing on a counteraction by some combination of interests which would be adversely affected.

No system was ever devised to accord so closely to a principle as ours was devised around Madison's theory of competition. We are a watchdog society. Both as a Congressional committee counsel and as Attorney General, I was a watcher, but I also was very definitely one of the watched. Professor Richard E. Neustadt of Columbia University, in his book *Presidential Power*, has observed that, as a result of the Founding Fathers, we are even now not a system of separated powers but a system of "separate institutions sharing power."

This principle of separated institutions, of watchful and jealous branches, extends beyond the mere formal institutions of government to the press, to the clergy and to all segments of society. When power corrupts and excesses continue for too long the system corrects itself. On countless occasions persons or groups outside of government act to check governmental actions and corrupt public officials. Fiorello La Guardia, New York City's great reform mayor, came to power on a wave of organized groups temporarily coalesced as the Fusion ticket. The two-party system is another case in point. Each party actually needs the other. Consider the more recent roles of the press, the Anti-Defamation

7

League and other service organizations, the churches, the NAACP and many other groups in exposing the deprivation of minority rights or the pockets of poverty existing in our affluent society. In each case private wrongs were exposed, government action was taken and the public spirit invigorated.

The second approach to the problem of power is as personal as the single human being who must hold great power and make great decisions in government, industry, the church and elsewhere. It is not as mechanical and automatic as the first, so that it is more difficult to achieve. Accordingly, success in its achievement varies with each generation, and it rests with all of us to take care that all who do rise to power are men and women who hold no interest higher than that of maintaining the system itself.

It is the essence of responsibility to put the public good ahead of personal gain. This still leaves room for individual goals and for the pursuit of them with energy and intelligence. This of course applies to daily life—to the family—as it does to politics. It simply requires that when men take on positions of high responsibility and enjoy the honors of high office they must be willing to relinquish something in return—their narrow self-interests.

Thus, we have nothing to fear from cooperative organization and authority lodged in government unless we fear individualism itself. I would encourage the many, rather than the few, to participate in public life at the national, state or local level. Along with this encouragement, however, I would add to the oath to support the Constitution an additional oath to be faithful to Madison's belief in the "diversity of the faculties of men" and that the "protection of those faculties is the first object of government." With that in our hearts how can we go wrong?

Underlying it all is the commitment of individual citizens to maintain individual and social freedom. Such responsibility was not a matter of choice in ancient Athens; it was a matter of duty. One could no more be a passive citizen than one could be a free slave. "Our ordinary citizens," said Pericles in his funeral oration, "though occupied with the pursuits of industry, are still fair judges of public matters . . . unlike any other nation, we regard him who takes no part in these duties not as unambitious, but as useless."

Today we cannot tolerate passive citizenship or passive commitment to freedom any more than could the father of the first democracy. If I saw anything in the last four years, it was that an individual can make an important contribution to the country whether in the Peace Corps or in some government office or in a community far removed from the center of power.

Jacqueline Kennedy said not long ago that "John Kennedy believed so strongly that one's aim should not just be the most comfortable life possible—but that we should all do something to right the wrongs we see and not just complain about them. He believed that one man can make a difference and that every man should try."

No amount of courage alone can make our system flourish. No army, however strong and watchful, alone can defend it. But if, on the other hand, our system is supported by the active will and commitment of all those who would remain free, then, however perilous the path, however great the obstacles, we can go forward confident that we will leave a better world for our children and our children's children.

Whatever secures for a man his own individuality is his unalienable right. And it was "to secure these rights," says the Declaration of Independence, that "Governments are instituted among Men." There should be no question about

9

the power or responsibility of government in our lives, but only the question of how it should be employed and what commitment each of us individually will make to maintain it. The challenge of politics and public service is to discover what is interfering with justice and dignity for the individual here and now, and then to decide swiftly upon the appropriate remedies.

In this book I have set forth the positions I took as Attorney General and the remedies I have felt to be most appropriate for some of the major problems of our time. Many subjects are not touched or are given only passing treatment, but I will be satisfied if the more detailed discussion of the problems herein contributes in a small way to a more meaningful political debate.

Upon leaving the practice of public law after thirteen years, and upon looking over the materials in this volume, I have had occasion to reflect upon what Burke would have called "the cause of our present discontents." The essential cause is poverty—poverty of goods and poverty of understanding. The consequences are loss of health, loss of dignity, loss of simple justice and loss of respect for law and order. While this may have been true of every age, there is a difference now, which is that for the first time in history we have every resource necessary to conquer all forms of poverty and their symptoms.

In America we already have conquered the problem of scarcity. Once that is accomplished, poverty is a problem not of production but of distribution. The poverty of goods is a matter of a more rational distribution at the forgotten margins of society; no massive redistribution is necessary. The poverty of understanding and of respect is a problem of university education and guidance in the rights and duties of man.

What I have to say in the pages that follow, and the reasons I have felt it necessary to speak out, can be summarized in a few short sentences:

I believe that, as long as there is plenty, poverty is evil. Government belongs wherever evil needs an adversary and there are people in distress who cannot help themselves.

I believe that, as long as the instruments of peace are available, war is madness. Government must be strong wherever madness threatens the peace.

I believe that, as long as most men are honest, corruption is twice vicious. It hurts men and it undermines their fundamental rights. We must be doubly wary, with private and public vigilance.

I believe that, as long as a single man may try, any unjustifiable barrier against his efforts is a barrier against mankind. A government that can destroy such a barrier without erecting any others in the process is a good force. A government too weak for that is not only a waste but an evil because it holds out false hope.

President Kennedy said, "Our problems are man made, therefore they can be solved by men. And man can be as big as he wants. No problem of human destiny is beyond human beings. Man's reason and spirit have often solved the seemingly insolvable—and we believe they can do it again." President Kennedy spoke on behalf of men's reason and spirit; he also acted for them. As free men and women, we can do no less.

ROBERT F. KENNEDY

New York, New York

Part II

SOCIETY AGAINST MEN

"Progress is a nice word. But change is its motivator. And change has its enemies."

CHAPTER 2

Federal Power and Local Poverty

Last year, on June 11, 1963, President Kennedy gave this description of a Negro child's birthright:

The Negro baby born in America today, regardless of the section of the nation in which he is born, has about one-half as much chance of completing high school as a white baby born in the same place on the same day, one-third as much chance of completing college, one-third as much chance of becoming a professional man, twice as much chance of becoming unemployed, about one-seventh as much chance of earning $10,000 a year, a life expectancy which is seven years shorter, and the prospects of earning only half as much.

Today that child is just over one year old. Have the odds in our communities changed for that child?

As public officials a major part of our task is to change those odds—to change them for *every* child, of whatever color, who is on the heavy side of the odds. When we talk about birthright we talk about the right of opportunity, *the right of opportunity to succeed or fail on individual*

15

talents developed unfettered by man-made barriers. That is what gives a man his dignity.

And opportunity denied or opportunity delayed—often one and the same—is not a question of color. One-tenth of our population is Negro. But a much larger proportion of our total population, closer to one-fifth, is poor.

Here is what the odds-makers would say of a white child born somewhere in a shack in the vast hills and valleys of despair we call Appalachia: Compared to other American youngsters the child would have about one-half the chance of completing the fifth grade. He or she would receive about half the educational dollars that are spent on the average American youngster. As a young adult the chances are twice as great that he or she would live in substandard housing and equally twice as great that he or she would eventually have to move from home for lack of work.

In one community I visited recently in one of the back hollows of West Virginia, there were forty families, but only three—only three—had fathers who were working. Ninety-five percent of the children were not in school, partially because a school bus could not get up the rutted road, and no effort had been made to arrange other transportation.

And those who were in school sat in a schoolhouse without running water, and without indoor plumbing; a school where books are out of date and worn, where the supply cabinet has little more than a box of pencils and a few crayons; a schoolhouse where the brightly colored food posters distributed by the National Dairy Council provide a contrast with the surplus commodities the youngsters had for dinner the night before.

Again, among the whites we need not single out Appalachia. All of us can think of examples in our own communities. Our cities contain neighborhoods in which the odds-makers would have no trouble ticking off the handicaps.

The storehouse that is accumulating these statistics is as explosive a container of unrest as any ghetto fenced by prejudice. In all of this there is one supreme problem and a dilemma for public policy and the political man.

The problem of poverty is the problem of the youth, whether they "hang around" at the side of a muddy road in West Virginia or on a street corner in Harlem. They can be found, differing only in number, in every city and hamlet in the United States.

The dilemma of poverty faced by the society and the polity is the gap between expectations and reality. Great expectations were the creation, not of idle political promises, but of the country itself and its history. We can no more change those high expectations than we can change our history. Therefore our only recourse is to change the opportunities for realizing the expectations. In this we have no choice, although all of us at one time or another have spoken and behaved as though we did.

There must be solutions to the dilemma of expectations rising against a static reality. To believe otherwise is to toss in the towel of social responsibility. I believe not only that there are appropriate remedies, but that they are ultimately to be found locally rather than nationally. The national government has ample constitutional power to enter into its war on poverty. This cannot be too strongly emphasized; and those who claim that the situation is or should be otherwise are usually found to be merely against a given program but lacking in the courage to say so. I say the solution will be local because national power, however broad in reach and however responsible in use, is severely limited in grasp. In the fight for social justice national power can create and encourage but local power is determinative.

National action is also not enough because the law is not enough. The right defined by law is not enough whether it concerns education or civil rights. We have a new civil rights law, and many of us live in states that have additional public accommodation and fair employment laws. But a decade of painful struggle for compliance must make us all wonder whether mere submission to the process of law is enough.

The mere presence of machinery—for civil rights or for idle youth and their impoverished parents—does not insure service. The fact that the structure exists has not insured its full use, and particularly its use to best advantage.

Recently in the capital, in the City of Washington, this lag of structure behind use was dramatically illustrated. We have many government and private agencies dedicated to relieving some of our severe social problems. More than a thousand families who live in what gently is called a "deteriorating neighborhood" were surveyed to learn how many had contact with our private and public social agencies. These were some of the findings:

Fewer than 5 percent of the families were involved with the Boy Scouts.

Fewer than 3 percent of the families were reached by the Boys Clubs.

Fewer than 3 percent had contact with the Salvation Army.

And one highly publicized settlement house reached three-tenths of one percent of the families.

The U.S. Employment Service reached about 11 percent; the PTA and other school groups, 9 percent; and only about 14 percent had any contact at all with churches.

Now the church, the Employment Service and the settlement house all were there. But again, this was not enough to reach the troubled youths and their parents in this neighborhood.

Today we have the new war on poverty and a host of expanded government services, all intent on bridging the gap between structure and use. While these will be debated and hammered into legislation on the Federal level, they will be organized and carried out by and in the communities.

The right to eat in a restaurant may be given Americans beneath the marble dome of Congress, but the food will be served up in obscure restaurants by friends and neighbors. A large part of a school dropout program may be financed out of a Federal office building, but the youngster will be chosen and helped by programs of distinctly local coloring.

Wherever dropout programs have worked, or job training has been successful, or educational approaches have been revised, in all these places we have found full political commitment. We have seen the political and business leadership of the community combine to back up the social worker, the youth leader and the teacher, who all have cried out about these problems for so long.

And they have worked.

We have proved again and again that important changes can be made in the deprived areas, that compliance to our social obligations can be meaningful.

Teachers have been trained to serve in the slums. And they have served well. Residents of impoverished areas have been called upon to help each other. And they have helped greatly. College youth have been recruited to teach their less affluent neighbors. And they have taught enthusiastically.

We have shown that IQs in the slums can rise rather than fall, that training programs provide jobs for the idle, and that new educational approaches provide hope for the previously hopeless.

Not long ago I was in Prince Edward County in Virginia to accept 9,964 pennies donated by children for the John F. Kennedy Library. For four years there were no schools at all in Prince Edward County. Youngsters who were ten and twelve years old formerly could not read the cover of a first-grade book. They read now. They do arithmetic now. They have meaningful education now.

Our task is to spread these achievements from the isolated to the general, from the test cases to all cases. The question facing us is: Can we combine all these isolated successes within a single community? Can we combine the established city leadership with the new leaders of the impoverished in an organized attack that will benefit both?

To organize our communities we need not bodies, but brains. We need not simply able bodies, but the best brains.

The hardest task is to appoint and incorporate in our work groups of men and women with the power and willingness to look at our community difficulties, dissect them, criticize areas of shortcoming and make meaningful suggestions.

Sometimes, too, it is hard to accept that sort of recommendation. For sometimes it carries with it announced or implied criticism of programs that have failed us in the past. Change means that someone's professional feathers will be ruffled, that a glass-topped desk might be moved to another office or abandoned, that pet programs might die.

Progress is a nice word. But change is its motivator. And change has its enemies.

The willingness to confront that change will determine how much we shall really do for our youth and how truly meaningful our efforts will be.

If we do this together, then that child born last year, that Negro child, that Appalachian child—and all children like them—will disappoint the odds-makers and the handicappers. And together we shall collect the winnings for having cheated failure and having glorified opportunity.

CHAPTER 3

Juvenile Delinquency: An Ounce
of Prevention

The New York City Police Athletic League is one of many
unselfish, dedicated civic organizations devoted to combating
juvenile delinquency. This year marks one-half century of
service since Police Captain John Sweeney brought PAL
into being in 1914, during the Administration of the youthful Mayor John Purroy Mitchel.

The minor delinquencies aimed at then seem innocuous
compared with the high crimes and misdemeanors committed
by juveniles today. We are impressed by the nature of our
problem when we are confronted with the fact that almost
half of the murderers in Death Row at Sing Sing are under
twenty-one. And the number of arrests of youths under
eighteen is increasing steadily. These might be totally dis-
couraging statistics if we did not have proof that modest
efforts on the part of the community, *if concerted,* can pay off
in enormously beneficial results. There are hundreds of thou-

sands of honorable and upright citizens who are alumni of PAL alone. The Sugar Ray Robinsons, the Phil Rizzutos, the Eddie Lopats, Louise Meads and Althea Gibsons are the personification of the great success governments and civic groups can have if they refuse to be discouraged.

But PAL and its counterparts everywhere also underscore the fact that the majority in the community *are* discouraged. One never finds more than a few hardy souls making a serious contribution to the war against the corruption of the youth. Today we are confronted with large increases in delinquency, particularly in major urban areas, and correlated with these increases is the high incidence of delinquency among minority groups. The results are disastrous, with the disintegration of many American families through either the inadequacy or the nonexistence of parents raising children in their own homes.

At the present time there are some two and a half million children who, for reasons beyond their control, are living outside their own family homes; and these, of course, are the children most susceptible to becoming delinquent or totally maladjusted. In 1960 the average number of youths aged sixteen to twenty-one who were out of school and out of work was a disturbing 450,000. But by last year, that number had grown to a whopping 700,000. They are forming the core of a new lost generation which is growing up in our country with no skills and little hope. Many of its members turn to the short cut of crime to get the things others get by hard work and study.

What is needed now is a systematized and intense effort to mobilize the resources of Federal, state and local governments and the private agencies, schools and churches which have done so much pioneer work. The Federal Government

23

ought to have a part in such programs, although ultimately it is up to city, state and private agencies to carry most of the load.

In 1961 two events occurred which have resulted in greater Federal action to deal with delinquency than ever before. First, the President established a Committee on Juvenile Delinquency and Youth Crime, composed of the Secretaries of Labor and Health, Education, and Welfare and myself as Attorney General, to coordinate and stimulate Federal delinquency programs. Second, Congress passed the Juvenile Delinquency Act, which authorized expenditure of thirty million dollars over a three-year period to test new approaches to delinquency prevention and control.

Crime, violence in the streets and the dissolution of families and personalities are not eliminated by calling them evil and blaming them on "some other" party. Nor are they eliminated by sloughing them off onto "some other" level of government. We begin by *accepting* the blame and the responsibility, not by displacing or disregarding them. Federal programs for delinquency prevention will work and should be expanded to help give the juvenile his birthright.

We have talked a lot about preventing delinquency but have not acted with equal vigor. Action rather than debate is what we need now. The facts are clear and threatening. We know that delinquency is growing faster every year, and at a rate faster than the youth population. We know that the big population jump in the age group from ten to twenty-one is just ahead. We have been warned repeatedly that our police, judicial and correctional facilities are inadequate to handle effectively the increasing number of law violations.

Despite these facts, our new expenditures, at all levels of government, are mainly for bigger enforcement and correctional programs. I do not object at all to more police, improved court procedures or more effective treatment facilities. Crime has to be repressed and communities must be protected. Offenders have to be controlled and reformed. The better we can do these jobs, the more chance we have of keeping first offenders from becoming hardened criminals. If we were successful in this alone, we could cut our national crime costs enormously.

But we should be pouring as much, or even more, money, manpower and imagination into preventing those early law violations that start criminal careers.

In the last thirty years much has been learned about detecting conditions which lead young people into criminal activities. In many communities large and small throughout the United States, some effective action is being taken. The knowledge and resources are scattered, however. The problem is to spread greater awareness of what is being done and what can be done; to increase the resources, particularly in trained personnel, for more effective action; and to bring such resources together in the same community. These tasks are the goals toward which the 1961 legislation will move us, but toward which we must move with greater speed and scope.

In the cases that come before the Department of Justice, involving a wide range of unlawful activities, we see repeated evidence of family and community failures.

For instance, there is the case of a young man now serving a term of twenty years in a Federal prison. From the age of nine he was involved in burglaries. He stole a gun at ten but was caught before he could use it. His offenses grew more serious. Probation, training schools and parole were tried by various agencies, but all these efforts failed. As a juvenile he was arrested ten times, made a ward of the court on two occasions and committed to correctional schools four times. He married at eighteen, but was not prepared to settle down. With his poor training he could get only temporary work as a common laborer. Before he was twenty-one, he had planned and executed several armed robberies.

In prison he was found to be nearly illiterate. In fact, previous institutions had classified him as having subnormal intelligence. However, in less than a year after incarceration, he completed elementary school.

Now he is doing well in the prison high school and making rapid progress in learning a trade as a skilled technician. Clearly enough, motivation and opportunity, not intelligence, had been missing before.

This case is striking because of the dramatic response to treatment. But there is nothing uncommon about the constructive potential in this young man that had never been tapped before. That part of the story could be duplicated in thousands of cases from the files in prisons and jails across the country.

The real tragedy in this particular case is that a Federal conviction for a major crime had to occur before an intensive effort was made to straighten out this young man's problems. How much better it would have been if the care and resources had been available to do the same thing for him at the age of nine or ten.

In this particular case, over a four-year period the proceeds of the crimes and the expense of arrest, conviction, confinement and treatment have cost society close to $100,000. Nor is this the end. He is not yet ready for release.

The more closely one looks at the cost and deployment of our crime prevention efforts, the more apparent it becomes that we have put too much responsibility at the end of the line, rather than at the beginning. Enforcement and correction can do only part of the job.

Costs for our Federal program of training, technical assistance and demonstration are now about ten million dollars a year. Contrast this request with figures on custodial care alone. A survey of 196 public and 78 private training schools in this country involving forty thousand children gives the following figures:

Current operating budgets run more than $61 million, and an additional $32 million a year are needed to bring services up to proper standards. Over a five-year period, it is estimated that another $135 million would be needed for capital improvements. In the Federal Bureau of Prisons budget, $6 million will be needed to replace the current facilities of the National Training School, which houses 450 boys. In the country-wide survey, the average annual cost of institutional services per child is about three thousand dollars, money enough, I might add, to pay his way in a university.

The Federal commitment to delinquency prevention in present and in contemplated legislation cannot compare with these costs. Clearly, an increased Federal role is not going to solve the problem either. But it can stimulate local community interest and investment in finding out how to do a better job of prevention. We can encourage development of programs that are effective and we can get this knowledge to those who need it.

We face a severe challenge. Daily before our eyes there is a growing army of unemployed and out-of-school youth. The challenge is to create new and meaningful opportunities for those young people. If we ignore this challenge, we invite the discontented and deprived to search for other solutions. I have seen some of the solutions:

There are the young hoodlums who think of nothing but getting into the rackets.

There are those who turn, instead, to theft, burglary and shoplifting as a career.

There are those unfortunates who become addicted to narcotics before they are out of their teens.

I have seen these young on the streets and in the prisons. I don't like what I have seen.

The job of providing constructive and challenging opportunities for young people throughout the nation is every citizen's business. This is not a matter for partisan political interest. We cannot say it is the responsibility of somebody else. It is not just a problem of inadequate parents in an indifferent community. Many families and communities show the effects of economic and racial discrimination beyond their control.

Nor can the residents of suburbs, rural areas and small towns attribute the problem to the corruption of the big city and refuse to help. Their children go to work and live in these cities in a steady migration. And the problems of the inner city have an infectious way of spreading outward. Mr. Hoover tells me that crimes are now increasing just as fast in rural areas and small towns as in the city. Back there in the inner city, where delinquency rates are still highest, is the place to stop this trend.

The Federal program is helping local communities find ways to aid young people before they are involved in serious trouble. The major changes in opportunities for young people will be achieved through basic legislation in the areas of education, housing and labor. However, with funds for delinquency prevention we are able to create new avenues by which the young people in trouble also can share in the expanding number of lawful opportunities.

There are many good programs already being tried in different parts of the country. There are many new ideas being proposed. Our job is to help put these scattered programs together so their full impact can be felt. In the President's Committee on Juvenile Delinquency and Youth Crime we had a means for mobilizing Federal resources to meet this challenge. Throughout the country we must continue to encourage agencies to get together to make these new programs work. This is important. We need to forget about personal interests or agency interests and get the job done.

Our goal is to assist local communities in their efforts to coordinate and develop their resources for preventing delinquency. The Federal Government can and must provide the leverage for work that no agency or community could ever hope to do alone.

CHAPTER 4

A Domestic Peace Corps—Satisfying the Ideal of Service*

We are all aware of, and delighted by, the success of the Peace Corps. The men and women who have served in it have brought to peoples around the world, in remote mountain villages and in bustling industrial cities, the true picture of the American of the sixties. It has been their spirit, their idealism, their skill and vitality which have done so much to erase the image of the "Ugly American."

I believe the same spirit, idealism, skill and vitality can be extremely helpful and effective in easing the plight of the Poor American and the Sick American. It could be a major step forward in strengthening the nation and its traditional concern for the worth of one individual.

* This statement on a "domestic peace corps" was delivered in May, 1963, as testimony before the special Subcommittee on Labor of the House Committee on Education and Labor. Over a year later Congress passed President Johnson's anti-poverty package, which included a domestic peace corps, called VISTA (Volunteers in Service to America). The testimony has been left unrevised and, except for some cutting, essentially as given. Since it helped shape and pass the legislation, the statement has some historical interest. But it also provides a set of standards and ideals by which the new VISTA ought to be organized and expanded.—Ed.

30

The "domestic peace corps" is a call to service. It is a challenge to people of all ages to follow the example of those in the Peace Corps: to serve their nation by helping other citizens to help themselves.

It is a challenge to youth. It is a challenge to millions of older and retired people whose reservoirs of skill and experience remain untapped. It is a challenge to all of our people to do more than merely talk about the ideal of service.

Every sixth citizen in the United States needs our help; there are five of us who should help him.

In early 1963 President Kennedy asked me to chair a Cabinet committee to determine whether the principle embodied in the Peace Corps could be applied effectively at home. This study has involved the attention of the Secretaries of Agriculture, Commerce, Labor, Interior and Health, Education, and Welfare, the Administrators of the Housing and Home Finance Agency and Veterans Affairs, and the Chairman of the Civil Service Commission. We also have been assisted by Mr. Shriver, the Director of the Peace Corps, and Mr. Gordon, Director of the Bureau of the Budget.

In the course of our study we visited a state hospital for the mentally retarded on a bright April day when you would have expected all the children to be playing outside. Not one was outside, nor was there a single child in either the well-equipped gymnasium or the classroom, well stocked with books.

The children were inside, standing in a room which was bare but for a few benches. The floor was covered with urine.

Severely retarded patients were left naked in cubicles, which suggested kennels, made of an elevated mattress enclosed on three sides by high marble slabs and covered on the fourth side by wire mesh so thick you could barely see through it.

31

Patients were washed by a device resembling a car wash—a spraying mechanism through which patients could be directed without the need for anyone to touch them. The only toilets for the approximately seventy patients in a large ward were located in the middle of the room, permitting no privacy. The hospital's hard-working but inadequate staff could provide at best only custodial care.

There is not even custodial care for great numbers of migratory farm workers, who live in almost unbelievable squalor.

At a Southwestern migratory labor camp one morning last month, a husband, his wife and their fourteen- and fifteen-year-old sons had to leave the camp at 4:30 A.M. in order to reach work in tomato fields thirty miles away. They had to leave their eleven-year-old daughter Sarah at home with three younger children because she has a crippled arm and cannot work in the fields.

All day, until the trucks came back from the fields at six in the evening, Sarah was responsible for three younger children, one seven, one four, and a sick baby six months old.

While she was fixing lunch for the children and trying to keep an eye on the baby, four-year-old Pete knocked a pan of boiling water off the oil burner, scalding his right leg and arm. His screams attracted an elderly woman in the next row of shacks. She did the best she could with home remedies. Nevertheless, within a day or so infection set in. Finally, Pete was taken to the County Hospital, but even after treatment he was left permanently crippled.

In another camp, cotton picking was over, after a season shortened by the introduction of mechanical cotton pickers. The last work the pickers had found was six weeks before, three hundred miles west, and then it was only for a short time.

One family of eleven people had been living in their car for three months. The mother and father slept in the car and two of the children were tucked into the trunk. The nine children ranged in age from three months to fourteen years.

The mother was seriously ill. The children were suffering from malnutrition and were unbelievably dirty because of the lack of sanitary facilities. All had been without food for several days. They had no money and virtually no hope; they did not know where to turn for help. Since they were not residents of the area their appeals were certain to be rejected.

These are not isolated examples.

Migratory Farm Workers

Of some 400,000 domestic migratory workers, 92,000 could find work for less than twenty-five days in 1960. The remainder, who worked more than twenty-five days, earned an average of $1,000 for the year. Those who worked less than twenty-five days received only $388.

Because of their constant movement from place to place following a harvest, migratory children fall years behind in education.

Alaskan Needs

In the Wade Hampton District of Alaska, which has a native population of three thousand, the median of school years completed is only 1.6. In Bethel the five thousand Alaskans average only a second-grade education.

Only 13 percent of the Alaskan rural natives have structurally sound housing. In Wade Hampton, which has 528 occupied homes, 476 are either deteriorating or dilapidating. None has a flush toilet. Only seven have hot and cold piped water. An average of four and a half persons occupy each room.

Alaskan natives on the average live only thirty years, compared with more than sixty-two years for the entire U.S. population.

Educational Needs

There are more than eight million Americans over twenty-five years of age who are illiterate. In 1960, 8.4 percent of our population twenty-five years or over had completed less than five years of school. More than one-fifth of our men fail the Selective Service preinduction mental exam.

Mortalities

It is still true that a nonwhite mother is four times as likely to die in childbirth as a white mother. There are 2.6 deaths per 10,000 live white births. The figure for nonwhites is 10.2 deaths.

Indians

The American Indian infant death rate is almost twice that of any other race in this country: 47 per 1,000 live births.

Life expectancy for Indians is forty-two years, twenty years less than for Americans as a whole.

I firmly believe that the "domestic peace corps" is a significant new means of attacking these problems. In the same way that thousands of our people have volunteered to serve in remote, dangerous and almost unknown corners of the world, we are convinced that Americans are equally willing to take on the toughest jobs in this country, whether in a city slum, an Indian reservation or a mining town.

The corps would consist of a small number of qualified, carefully trained Americans chosen for their skill and their quality. It would provide an opportunity for these people to offer themselves full time to work with fellow Americans who are in need. Corpsmen would not be technical assistance experts. The program would not be service *to* people, but working *with* people.

The corps could call the attention of the nation to the plight of invisible millions, and illustrate that the needs of the deprived are not only the special interest of a few dedicated professions, but a deep national interest.

Specifically, what would the corpsmen do? Many local groups are so enthusiastic about the prospects for this program that they have written detailed appeals for corpsmen. Already, we have received so many requests that even the corps at full strength could not fulfill them all. One example will demonstrate what I mean.

The San Carlos Apache Tribal Council of the Arizona counties of Gila, Graham and Pinal has asked for six corpsmen to live with the tribe. Seventy-five percent of these tribe members are unemployed. Half the families receive less than five hundred dollars a year in income. Housing conditions are desperate. Two rooms house fourteen for eating, sleeping and cooking. The houses are cold in the winter and so hot in summer that people must live outdoors. There is no running water.

Two of the six corpsmen would be general construction workers, experienced in plumbing, wiring, carpentry and masonry, who would help in the construction and maintenance of homes. One would be a farm assistant with knowledge of family agriculture to teach techniques of animal husbandry, family gardening, small machinery maintenance and repair. Two corpsmen would teach reading, writing and accounting skills to adults. The sixth corpsman would be an assistant to work with families on nutrition, infant care, preservation of food and home medical care.

As a companion effort, corpsmen would help train others to teach these subjects so that corpsmen would, after a period of time, be able to turn their duties over to local volunteers. Each corpsman would take the lead in instituting recreation and productive group activities.

This is one example of what six corpsmen could do. The story could be paralleled in hundreds of different places in this country where persons are in critical need.

The corps would not compete with existing groups or displace them. It would consult and cooperate with interested local service groups, and in this sense the program would be a tribute to the great numbers of Americans working on these problems in their own communities. At the same time, it would attract many more people to the service professions, most of which badly need personnel.

That is not to say that the social agencies, the psychologists, the psychiatrists, the mental institutions and all the other forces which operate for the general good are to be "somehow supplanted" by, let us say, a young man or woman or a retired person who wishes to give a helping hand. The professional societies are central to the concept of the corps; they endorse the corps enthusiastically. Once again, their endorsement demonstrates the need of people to serve as well as the need of those who must be served.

While corpsmen would work with people in many settings and at varied tasks, every project must meet two conditions. First, it must provide for work with the people who most need help. Corpsmen would not be sent to localities which have sufficient local resources and programs. They would concentrate on the "pockets" of need where there are not sufficient people or resources.

Second, it would be inappropriate and destructive to superimpose this program over local community efforts. A new bureaucracy must not be built. Work must be done through existing state and local agencies and institutions. The corps would consider projects only at local request—only after a locality had specifically invited corpsmen to perform jobs that had been clearly defined.

The local request would have to be a basic statement, not of what the community wanted to get for free from the government, but of how it would use the people this program will provide. Consistent with the purpose of stimulating increased volunteer efforts at the local level, each project request would have to present a plan for the phasing out of corpsmen.

The demand for this program is clearly demonstrated by the expressions already received from state and local, public and private organizations serving migratory workers, Indians, residents of depressed or isolated rural areas or of urban slums, and persons cared for in institutions.

That there are a great many people who would and could serve in the program is equally clear. The analyses of recruitment showed overwhelming support by the two groups which would supply most of the corpsmen—college students and retired persons. We have tested the appeal with those in the overseas Peace Corps and find that even after two years of service abroad a significant number would serve in a domestic corps.

Our surveys and the conclusions of prominent scholars in these fields show that a tenth of our population is fallow. Millions of Americans who have years of productivity and service to offer are dormant. Retired teachers, craftsmen and tradesmen really don't want to go to the seashore to fade away. They want to help. So many of these people have come forward that I am convinced they can accomplish something unique in this country, something undone by all the Federal, state, county and private agencies, something still to be done.

The tradition on which this program depends is one of the basic strengths of our nation. That is the tradition of helping your neighbor. We are by nature hospitable and generous. In our colonial period everyone was a volunteer. This voluntaryism is alive today. It finds a magnificent example in the men and women of the Peace Corps, but it is present here at home as well.

In 1958 New York's Metropolitan Hospital initiated an experiment in the use of teen-age volunteers. The first contingent of volunteers was to be recruited by radio announcements. As a result of the announcements, one thousand teen-agers applied for fifty volunteer openings.

In the summer of 1961 the Junior Red Cross of New York had 2,400 teen-age volunteers working in one hundred vacation playgrounds and forty-nine city voluntary and veterans hospitals in the New York area.

The American people have repeatedly and heroically responded to their country's call in wartime. There has been little demand that they also serve in time of peace. But just as our people have volunteered to serve in remote corners of the world, they are now willing to assume equally difficult jobs in this country, whether on an Indian reservation, in a big-city slum or in a mental hospital.

This program asks Americans to invest a year of their lives, at no salary and under Spartan conditions, to help millions of their fellow citizens who, through no fault of their own, are denied the essentials of a decent life.

I am proud to admit that this concept is idealistic.

Part III

MEN AGAINST SOCIETY

*". . . every society gets the
kind of criminal it deserves . . .
[and] the kind of law enforcement it insists on."*

CHAPTER 5

Eradicating Free Enterprise in Organized Crime

> "The American system of ours, call it Americanism,
> call it capitalism, call it what you like, gives each and
> every one of us a great opportunity if we only seize it
> with both hands and make the most of it."

While the philosophy expressed in the above quotation may
be spotless, its author was Al Capone. And in the thirty-five
years since it was uttered, too many "independent businessmen" have sought literally to "make the most of it."

Organized crime, one of the biggest businesses in America,
has many faces. Some are well known, like that of the gambler
operating the roulette wheel which is not only illegal, but
fixed. Another is that of the narcotics peddler, trading on the
misery of the poor. There are other faces—those of racketeers
who engage in extortion, prostitution, corrupt labor relations
and bootlegging.

The reason racketeering can flourish in our society depends, however, on some other faces not so well known. There is the rackets leader, seeking protection from the law, and there is the public official who offers it, for a price, daily betraying his position of honor and trust in his community. There is the syndicate gunman who issues threats, and there is the potential witness who receives them, frightened almost inevitably into silence.

It is this last aspect which makes the job of fighting racketeering hardest, and it is this aspect which means that one of our most important weapons in the fight, at the Federal and local level, is criminal intelligence. Intelligence, the most detailed information obtainable on the background and activities of suspected criminals, is essential to all law enforcement. It is even more important to successful action against racketeers.

Evidence concerning their clandestine operations is particularly hard to uncover. A witness who will testify in the face of threats to himself and his family is rare. This is one reason the disclosures made by Joseph Valachi are significant: for the first time an insider, a knowledgeable member of the racketeering hierarchy, has broken the underworld's code of silence.

Valachi's disclosures are more important, however, for another reason. In working a jigsaw puzzle, each piece in place tells us something about the whole picture and enables us to see additional relationships. It is the same in the fight against organized crime. Valachi's information is a significant addition to the broad picture. It adds essential detail and brings the picture into sharper focus. It gives meaning to much that we already know.

The picture is an ugly one. It shows what has been aptly described as a private government of organized crime, a government with an annual income of billions, resting on a base of human suffering and moral corrosion.

In 1957 more than a hundred top racketeers met at the now infamous crime convention at Apalachin, New York. But until 1960 the Federal Government had only the barest shreds of evidence about what happened at that meeting. A number of the delegates, including those from Chicago, escaped detection. Federal investigative agencies are now pooling information on more than eleven hundred major racketeers. Because of the investigative vigilance possible as a result of this intelligence effort, such a meeting could not occur unobserved today.

Because of intelligence gathered from Joseph Valachi and from other informants:

We know that Cosa Nostra is run by a Commission and that the leaders of Cosa Nostra in most major cities are responsible to the Commission. We know that membership in the Commission varies between nine and twelve active members, and we know who the active members of the Commission are today.

We know that in the past two years at least three carefully planned Commission meetings had to be called off because the leaders learned that we had uncovered their well-concealed plans and meeting places.

We know that the Commission makes major policy decisions for the organization, settles disputes among the "families" and allocates territories of criminal operation within the organization. For example, we now know that the meeting at Apalachin was called by a leading racketeer in an effort to resolve the problem created by the murder of Albert Anastasia. The racketeer was concerned that Anastasia had brought too many individuals not worthy of membership into the organization. To insure the security of the organization, the racketeer wanted these men removed. Of particular concern to this racketeer was the fact that he had violated Commission rules in causing the attempted assassination of Frank Costello, deposed New York rackets boss, and the murder of Anastasia. He wanted Commission approval for these acts—which he received.

We know that the Commission now has before it the question of whether to intercede in the Gallo-Profaci family gangland war in New York. Gang wars produce factionalism, and continued factionalism in the underworld produces sources of information to law enforcement. Indications are that the gangland leaders will resolve the Gallo-Profaci fight.

The casualty list of this one gang war alone offers a somber illustration of how cruel and calculating the underworld continues to be. Since the summer of 1961 there have been five persons murdered and thirteen persons seriously injured. Ten of these were shot, one nearly strangled, one beaten in a New York night club, and one beaten and then thrown from a speeding car. Such violence is not limited to New York. There have been thirty-seven gangland murders since 1960 in Chicago, and in the Youngstown, Ohio, area there have been seventy bombings since 1950.

We know that Joseph Magliocco, who has taken over in Brooklyn as successor to the recently deceased Joseph Profaci, has not been confirmed by the Commission and will probably not be. This is despite the fact that Magliocco recently sought the support of Commission members Angelo Bruno and Steve Maggadino.

We know that while Vito Genovese is in Federal prison Tommy Eboli is substituting for him in New York and Gerry Catena is doing the same in New Jersey. Because of the power that Genovese wielded within the organization and the fear in which he is held by the New York organization, no move has been made to take over the top spot while his appeal of a narcotics conviction is pending in the courts. If Genovese stays in prison after his case is concluded, we anticipate a major underworld power struggle in New York.

We know that because of Federal intelligence efforts other Commission meetings have been limited to one or two members and have been held in highly clandestine fashion.

Such intelligence is important not only because it can help us learn what to watch for, but because of the assistance it can provide in developing and prosecuting specific cases. Syndicate leaders and their associates have been identified, and all are now under intensive investigation. A number of major racketeering figures have been convicted, and many more cases are in the indictment or investigation stage.

Thus we have been able to make inroads into the hierarchy, personnel and operations of organized crime. It would be a serious mistake, however, to overestimate the progress Federal and local law enforcement has made. A principal lesson provided by the disclosures of Joseph Valachi and other informants is that the job ahead is very large and very difficult.

We are doing an increasingly better job of using most of our assets in the effort to curb the enormous power of organized crime. But the effort has only begun. In 1961 and 1962 Congress granted us new statutory authority with which to act against the rackets. With bipartisan concern and support, we obtained new laws forbidding interstate travel for racketeering purposes, interstate shipment of gambling machines or paraphernalia, and use of interstate communications for gambling purposes.

These statutes have given the FBI jurisdiction to investigate such activity for the first time. Further, the FBI's investigative jurisdiction has been enlarged with the expansion of the Fugitive Felon and Federal Firearms Acts.

With these additional legal weapons, we have been able to improve greatly the Federal law enforcement effort. The Organized Crime and Racketeering Section of the Department's Criminal Division has been enlarged and revitalized, and it has been given increasingly powerful help in prosecuting cases from the various Federal investigative agencies.

The statistics for cases involving organized crime give some indication of our activity. For the first six months of 1963, we secured indictments of 171 racketeering figures, compared with 24 for the same period three years ago. In 1963 the number of convictions was 160; three years before it was 35.

Organized-crime cases have been in large part responsible for sharp increases in the work figures for the entire Criminal Division. In 1962 Criminal Division attorneys spent 809 days in court and 7,359 days in the field. Two years prior, the figures were 283 days in court and 1,963 days in the field.

The parallel efforts of the investigative agencies have been unremitting. Above and beyond its outstanding activity under previous statutes, the FBI has conducted extensive and effective investigations of possible violations of the new laws. It is penetrating deeply into the operations and structure of the rackets.

The Federal Bureau of Narcotics has continued and improved on its notable record of intelligence-gathering and enforcement. The Internal Revenue Service is pursuing racketeer tax frauds as an integral and important part of its work. The Immigration and Naturalization Service, Postal Inspectors and Customs Bureau, the Secret Service, the Department of Labor and other agencies all have made an important contribution to our effort.

The work of local law enforcement officials in many communities has been outstanding, notably in Los Angeles under Police Chief Wiliam Parker, in Cincinnati under Police Chief Stanley R. Schrotel and in New York under Commissioner Michael J. Murphy.

All these efforts notwithstanding, we have yet to exploit properly our most powerful asset in the battle against the rackets: an aroused, informed and insistent public.

In the words of the old saying, every society gets the kind of criminal it deserves. What is equally true is that every community gets the kind of law enforcement it insists on. Regardless of new laws and old, regardless of resourceful and dedicated Federal investigative efforts, and regardless of how well rounded a picture of organized crime our intelligence helps us to secure, the only force that can conquer organized crime is the vigilance of citizens in every community.

Public attention has not, of course, been sufficient, because it has not been sufficiently vigilant and organized. The extensive efforts of the McClellan Committee* and those of the late Senator Kefauver† focused attention on the problem. And investigative and enforcement agencies at all levels are working harder than ever. Yet not only has organized crime not diminished; it has become an even more urgent national problem.

As I testified before the Senate and House Judiciary Committees in the summer of 1961, we estimated that illegal gambling alone had a gross volume of some seven billion dollars annually. We have made progress since that time. But there is no doubt that illegal gambling still takes in enormous amounts of money, much of which is used to feed other kinds of organized crime.

* This is the Permanent Investigations Subcommittee of the Senate Government Operations Committee.—Ed.

† The Special Committee to Investigate Organized Crime in Interstate Commerce, U.S. Senate, 1950-51.—Ed.

To illustrate: in an interstate numbers game case which we prosecuted successfully in New York City, records seized during a raid disclosed that this single operation grossed six million dollars a year. In the three related cases successfully prosecuted in the Western District of Pennsylvania, a total of forty million dollars was involved.

Figures of this magnitude have been found all over the country. In the state of Washington the defendants in a case involving interstate transportation of pinball machines admitted in open court that they paid 20 percent of their gross income of $16.5 million to the state in taxes in thirty months despite the fact that the pinball machines, which were the source of the money, were illegal under state law.

Narcotics also provide enormous profits. Because of the remarkable vigilance and law enforcement efforts of the Bureau of Narcotics, under Henry Giordano, we know the syndicate leadership has ordered its members to stay out of the narcotics traffic. The greed of a number of racketeers is so great, however, that despite the risk and despite these orders they have continued to operate extensively in this field. More than a score of Cosa Nostra members have been convicted recently on narcotics charges.

This greed and the efforts of the Bureau of Narcotics are typified by a historic case involving an international heroin ring. This operation smuggled, conservatively speaking, $150 million worth of heroin into this country in the false bottoms of trunks supplied to unsuspecting Italian immigrants.

How important this case was to the syndicate can be gauged from what happened to the twenty-four men indicted in New York. The body of one defendant was found in the Bronx, full of bullet holes, shortly before the trial. The badly burned body of a second defendant was found in a field near Rochester, New York, during the trial. Another defendant attempted suicide, and three others, the leaders of the ring here, fled the country, two of them forfeiting fifty thousand dollars' bail. The Bureau of Narcotics, picking up their trail in the Caribbean, traced them to Italy and then to Spain, where they were arrested, and returned them to this country. Ultimately, they were convicted both on the original narcotics charges and also on flight charges. The remaining defendants were convicted and sentenced to long prison terms.

Gambling and narcotics are not the only sources of great income to the rackets. Usurious loans, known in the underworld as "juice loans" or "shylocking," involve large amounts, as well as frequent hoodlum threats of violence made to insure repayment. Considering that an interest rate of six dollars back for five borrowed per week is not unusual in the underworld, the size of the profits from this activity is apparent. If there is no repayment, that rate would compound to more than 700 percent over the usual twelve-week loan period.

Yet even the enormous amounts of money involved in these activities tell only part of the story of the rackets' financial interests. What is at least as disturbing, and far more insidious, is the increasing encroachment of the big businessmen of the rackets upon legitimate business.

In some cases the familiar weapon of extortion has been used not only as a source of direct income, but as a wedge to obtain control of respectable enterprises. An illuminating case in point began in 1960 with a series of threats directed against the partners in a Brooklyn furniture enterprise. Subsequently, one partner was beaten by unknown assailants. Acting on the advice of a New York rackets leader, the partners then sought protection from another important racketeer who ranked high in the Profaci-Magliocco family.

The "patron" agreed to provide the necessary protection, but announced that he, too, was now a partner in the business, of which the paid-up inventory alone was more than sixty thousand dollars. In return for his new "partnership" he gave ten thousand dollars to one partner for his entire interest and five thousand dollars to the other for a half-interest. Thereafter, the racketeer proceeded to milk the company dry. Then came a series of mysterious fires which resulted in an insurance settlement of over $105,000.

Another scheme used by racketeers for intrusion into legitimate business is bankruptcy fraud. The method of operation is simple, and racketeer involvement in such cases is increasing. A racketeer buys or opens a retail store, often through a "front" man. He deposits substantial funds into a bank account for the store and, using that as a basis for credit, orders large amounts of merchandise. He then sells the goods through the ostensibly legitimate store, but does not pay his creditors. Anxious to protect their investment, they give him extended opportunity to pay. By the time the collector comes with the sheriff, however, the ostensible merchant has disappeared—or contends that he lost the retail sale proceeds, now safely hidden, at the race track or in a so-called burglary.

Still another form of encroachment upon legitimate business is the fictitious employee scheme. To cloak their illegal activities, racketeers in some parts of the country have arranged to be placed on the payrolls of ostensibly legitimate businesses, which they may, indeed, own themselves. This employment is purely fictitious, and the racketeer performs no services for the firm. But the "job" permits him to devote his time to operating illegal activities, while the job title and his tax returns show him to be a member of the honest business community.

A racketeer in this position can use the business as a funnel for racketeering profits by repaying loans, for example, with illegally obtained funds. This kind of activity has been under scrutiny in several areas, including a Midwestern city where nine top racketeers are engaged in fictitious "front" jobs.

Other racketeers have interests in a variety of legitimate businesses: the garment industry, construction, bowling alleys, liquor wholesaling, real estate, jukeboxes, vending machines, restaurants and others.

Such business interests in some cases have fostered official corruption. In an Eastern city a leading racketeer and the city's mayor and police chief are awaiting trial on charges of extensive corruption involving substantial pay-offs to the city officials in exchange for approving contracts for city business.

In a Midwestern city a high-ranking municipal official is under indictment for attempting to extort thousands of dollars from firms seeking city contracts. There are other, similar cases, and we now have more than a hundred investigations in thirty states involving the corruption of public officials.

Another highly profitable activity for racketeers with legitimate business interests has been stock fraud. Often, rackets figures with considerable capital at their disposal invest, not only in legitimate securities, but also in questionable stock. Typically, they artificially raise the price of such stock with calculated purchases and then sell large amounts through "boiler room" telephone solicitation. In one case a leading Eastern rackets figure is now under indictment for evading taxes on more than a million dollars' profit received from such sale of stock.

Similar situations and cases involving the sale of stolen securities are now under close investigation.

Racketeers' intrusions into business are paralleled by their intrusions into labor relations. In the one thousand days of the Kennedy-Johnson Administration prosecutive action was taken against a number of corrupt businessmen as well as dishonest officers or members of some forty-five different unions.

During that time, forty-three labor and thirty-four management representatives were indicted for violations of the Taft-Hartley Act prohibition against pay-offs to union officials. A total of 201 persons were indicted for this and other labor-management offenses during the same period, and we have so far secured 146 convictions.

In the case of the International Brotherhood of Teamsters alone, in the same period we secured 124 indictments against union officers, members and associates and, up to that point, had secured sixty-five convictions, with seven acquittals. In addition, as the result of Federal-local cooperation, there were twenty-three convictions on state charges.

The job of law enforcement has become correspondingly harder as racketeering figures have tried to blur the line, in all fields, between their criminal and legitimate activities.

Our principal problem is insulation. The kingpins of the rackets, our main targets, are often far removed from their illegal activities. In fact, when we see that one of our subjects has become operational, we know he is no longer a kingpin.

For example, a rackets lord need only contact one or two trusted lieutenants to successfully direct a massive, illegal gambling operation and collect great profits. With modern means of communication, he need not even enter the state in which the illegal activity is centered. Needless to say, the racketeer knows that under present law his telephone conversations are protected from interference.

And there are various telephone techniques to frustrate investigating officers, who must attempt to obtain evidence of violations legally. A bookmaker may subscribe to a regular telephone answering service. A bettor calls, usually from a pay phone, and leaves his number. The bookmaker then calls the answering service periodically and places telephone calls from pay booths to his customers. Gamblers also install hidden "knife" switches or similar devices which can be tripped to cut the telephone circuit and prevent raiding officers from accepting calls from bettors which come in after they have gained entrance to the gambler's premises.

Top racketeers always deal in cash, and there are innumerable ways to conceal cash from the very best of investigators. Secret numbered accounts in foreign banks, legitimate "front" businesses of the kind I have described, loan sharking—these are but a few methods.

Organized crime not only becomes more refined in its activities, but also takes advantage of modern developments in transportation and communication. As it does so, and grows richer and more powerful in the process, it can more easily elude law enforcement efforts.

And as evidence becomes harder to obtain, the importance of informants increases correspondingly. They, to say the least, are hard to come by. The usual reply of a convicted hoodlum in a position to give information is that he doesn't want to trade a jail cell for a hearse.

But even the increasing flow of information from such sources as Joseph Valachi does not answer the problem. Being able to identify a top racketeer is one thing. Securing the evidence to convict him in a court of law is quite another.

While the new legal weapons Congress has already provided have been extraordinarily effective, as I indicated earlier, additional legislation is needed. First, Congress should provide authority to guarantee immunity to witnesses testifying in racketeering investigations. Second, it should reform and revise the wiretapping law.

The problem of obtaining testimony is nowhere more acute than in establishing violations of the racketeering travel act (Section 1952 of Title 18, United States Code, interstate and foreign travel or transportation in aid of racketeering enterprises), which the Congress enacted in August, 1961. Immunity here would materially assist our investigations of interstate racketeering in gambling, liquor, narcotics, prostitution, extortion and bribery. For example, the power of immunity under the bribery provision of this statute could be used to advantage in our investigations of political corruption.

To assist still further our investigations of political corruption, which is such a serious by-product of organized criminal activity, Congress should also provide for the use of immunity in the general bribery and conflict-of-interest statutes. In the Eighty-eighth Congress this was embodied in S. 1246, and this bill should be passed. This change would make an important tool available in certain political corruption situations where we are unable to establish an interstate connection as required under the travel statute.

Finally, if we are to make maximum progress in our drive on organized crime, I am convinced that we need legislation to permit the use of wiretapping by law enforcement officials. The urgency for revision of the present and ineffective provisions of the wiretapping statute is emphasized by the fact that the latest electronic improvements are easily available to the criminal. The advantages these can give him over law enforcement officers are plain. Leading racketeers make almost unrestricted use of interstate facilities, particularly communications, to direct their illegal activities.

Here lies the anomaly: the present statute fails to protect the right of privacy over the telephone, because anyone can *listen in* without violating that statute. At present, to convict someone of illegal wiretapping, we must prove not only that a tap was made, but also that there was unlawful disclosure of the conversation. At the same time, disclosure *by Federal officers* of evidence gained from wiretapping violates Federal law.

Compare the following two examples: *

1. In 1959, while inspecting a fire-alarm station, the fire chief of a large Western city made a startling discovery. The recording system had been rigged to record not only fire-alarm calls but also all calls on the chief's private line. The chief looked further. He found a recording tape on which was transcribed a personal telephone conversation between himself and a United States Senator.

The Department of Justice discovered the identity of the wiretapper but was forced to close the file on this case without having taken any action against him. He could not be prosecuted under the present Federal wiretapping statute, which should protect against such gross invasion of individual privacy, but does not.

2. Last fall, District Attorney Frank Hogan of New York City developed a strong case against seven of the top narcotics distributors in the country, men who had operated a multimillion-dollar narcotics ring in the New York City area for

* The following four paragraphs appeared in *The New York Times Magazine*, June 3, 1962, under the title "Attorney General's Opinion on Wiretaps," by Robert F. Kennedy. © 1962 by The New York Times Company. Reprinted by permission.

more than five years. Yet on November 14 Mr. Hogan abandoned his prosecution of the seven men. Much of his evidence came from wiretapping and, although the wiretaps had been authorized by a court, as is permissible in New York, he felt he could not introduce this evidence without committing a Federal crime.

In other words, the men could not be prosecuted because of the present Federal wiretapping statute, which should permit reasonable use of wiretapping by responsible officials in their fight against crime, but does not.

Thus the present law neither prevents indiscriminate wiretapping nor recognizes the legitimate needs of law enforcement for authority, closely circumscribed, to use this means of gathering evidence.

In 1963 the Department of Justice resubmitted to the Congress a carefully worded bill, S. 1308, with strong procedural safeguards, which would afford a clear-cut basis for the legitimate and controlled use of wiretapping by law enforcement officials. At the same time, the bill would expressly forbid all other types of wiretapping.

Section 5(b) of this bill empowers the Attorney General, or an Assistant Attorney General specially designated by the Attorney General, to authorize application to a Federal judge for a wiretap order. The section empowers the judge to issue an order permitting wiretapping in cases involving national security, murder, kidnaping and racketeering cases.

If one thing is clear, it is that organized crime is a national problem. The racketeer is not someone dressed in a black shirt, white tie and diamond stickpin, whose activities affect only a remote underworld circle. He is more likely to be outfitted in a gray flannel suit, and his influence is more likely to be as far-reaching as that of an important industrialist.

The American public may not see him, but that makes the racketeer's power for evil in our society even greater. Lacking direct confrontation with racketeering, the American citizen is all too likely to fail to see the reason for alarm.

The reason, decidedly, exists. The financial cost of organized crime is not limited to the vast illicit profits of gambling or narcotics. When racketeers bore their way into legitimate business, the cost is borne by the public.

When the infiltration is into labor relations, the racketeer's cut is paid by higher wages and higher prices—in other words, by the public.

When the racketeer bribes local officials and secures immunity from police action, the price exacted by corrupt law enforcement, incalculable in dollars, is paid, again, by the public.

CHAPTER 6

White-Collar Crimes: "Antitrust Is Probusiness"

Mark W. Cresap, president of Westinghouse, a firm, incide
tally, which was a defendant in the electrical equipme
[price-fixing] case, recently said: "Government is not t
enemy of business; business is not the enemy of governme1
There is only one enemy and we know who it is."

On May 5, 1961, I delivered a Law Day address at the U1
versity of Georgia Law School in Athens, Georgia. At tl
time I said:

You may ask, will we enforce the civil rights statutes? The ¡
swer is, "Yes, we will." We will also enforce the antitrust laws, t
antiracketeering laws, the laws against kidnaping and robbi
Federal banks and transporting stolen automobiles across st:
lines, the illicit traffic in narcotics and all the rest. . . . I holc
constitutional office of the United States Government, and I sh
perform the duty I have sworn to undertake: to enforce the l¿
in every field of law, without regional bias or political slant.

58

This was the underlying philosophy of my actions in the Department of Justice. It was our policy in every field, including enforcement of the antitrust laws.

The Kennedy-Johnson Administration has not been anti-business primarily because there is every good reason why we should be probusiness. Furthermore, I might add that I look upon the antitrust laws as being "probusiness." I believe firmly that the purpose of the antitrust laws is to protect and promote the competitive interests of business, small and large, as well as to protect the public.

Fortune Magazine several years ago stated that proposition extremely well:

> Now that socialism and planning have failed wherever they have been tried abroad, it is all the more necessary that Americans look to those institutions which have tended to preserve their own flexible, dynamic and competitive society . . . whatever the difficulties that surround the enforcement of the Sherman Act today, it remains, in the words of former Chief Justice Hughes, a charter of freedom standing for something precious in American life.

This statement correctly declares what the antitrust laws are.

Yet there is talk that enforcement of the antitrust laws is evidence that the Administration has been "antibusiness." Much of the criticism has centered on merger cases brought under Section 7 of the Clayton Act. This section is intended to avoid the creation of barriers to entry into the market and the loss of competitive vigor which may result through excessive concentration in a particular industry. It is not intended to prevent all mergers. Many mergers promote vigorous competition just as some mergers have the opposite effect.

The record shows that mergers have not been attacked indiscriminately. The number of mergers challenged by the government is very small compared with the total number

59

of mergers which are completed. During the first eight months of 1961 the Department filed only eleven antimerger cases. In the same period 757 mergers or acquisitions were recorded by the Federal Trade Commission. Included in the mergers we opposed were five bank mergers.

This takes us into a category where there is a great deal of controversy and criticism. I have seen it written and heard it argued that we should not have challenged any bank mergers; that they are not covered by Section 7 of the Clayton Act; and that since these mergers had been approved by other government agencies, including the Comptroller of the Currency, we had no business getting into this field.

I will not attempt to win the legal argument here. However, there are some points that should be made clear from the record. For example, during my first year as Attorney General the Department of Justice examined some 155 bank mergers. Of those, we disapproved of only five. And when we disapproved, it did not come like a bolt out of the blue to the banks concerned. I did not assume the office of Attorney General and at once say, "Let's attack all bank mergers."

Bank mergers have been a matter of concern to the Antitrust Division since 1955. Several large mergers were under study by the Eisenhower Administration, and in at least one instance a bank merger was abandoned because antitrust action was contemplated. Several suits were filed attacking proposed bank mergers, and early in my tenure we took action in five cases on the basis of recommendations of officials who had been studying this problem long before I became Attorney General. Furthermore, the banks involved in these five cases had been notified, prior to their merger, that the Department of Justice probably would disapprove.

So these actions did not come as a surprise to the banks

as I have seen some writers contend. In one case we informed the banks of our opposition, and they merged early one morning before we could take any legal action to prevent it. In another case we went to court to obtain an injunction opposing the merger. The judge, out of courtesy, notified the banks' lawyers. The lawyers thereupon hurriedly completed the merger within the next few minutes in an attempt to defeat our efforts. These are actions that the bank officials and their lawyers had a right to take. I have no criticism. But it is difficult to see how the Federal Government can be criticized as being unfair or unreasonable in seeking to have legitimate legal questions determined in the court and, if we are right, in seeking to have the banks returned to their original state.

An editor of a prominent business magazine wrote in this connection that business is friendless in Washington these days and cited the following example. He said: "Let a few banks get permission from proper Governmental authorities to merge and what happens? Another branch of Government rushes in to stop the action—either by hastily-planned gobbledy-gook, or by time-worn courtroom gimmicks."

That statement is just not in accordance with the facts. But the businessman reading the article cannot know the background, and so to him, because of ignorance or lack of knowledge, Washington becomes "antibusiness." For example, in the early days of our Administration a publisher of a large magazine which frequently points out that a Democratic Administration is "antibusiness" called me. He said that we could avoid antibusiness feeling if we would permit firms which are planning to merge to obtain an indication from the Department of Justice as to whether their action would result in an antitrust lawsuit. He proposed that we put such a practice into effect. I pointed out to him that this practice had been in existence for the whole time since I h; been Attorney General and for many years prior. His answ was that businessmen perhaps didn't understand and th we should get this information out to the public.

I believe, however, that despite misunderstandings the are still many businessmen who recognize that the Depai ment of Justice has a role to play in helping and protectii them. Sometimes I wish these gentlemen were more artic late. They have solid facts to which they could refer.

Taking just one five-month period, the Antitrust Divisic received 439 complaints of antitrust violations. Two-thir of these, almost three hundred, came from businessmen, ar these complaints covered almost every conceivable cor modity, from concrete pipes and corrugated boxes to ro salt, waste paper, drugs, milk and meat. The list demonstrat that there is probably no area of the business communi which has not at one time or another sought the Department assistance.

Complaints have come, not just from small- or middle-si; businessmen, but from big business as well. The history antitrust law enforcement shows that successful antitru prosecutions have often strengthened and brought vitality extremely large companies and businesses. We have take some actions involving big business either because con petitors were engaged in predatory activities or because se eral competitors were planning a merger which could stif competition.

Take such a predatory act as price-fixing by big busines The Sherman Act has been on the books since July 2, 189 The Clayton Act became law on October 15, 1914. Howeve the fact that seven top executives in the electrical industi went to jail brought home for the first time to many Amer cans that there are laws to prevent companies from banding together in secret to rig prices, to fix bids and to stifle competition.

I regard price-fixing violations such as those in the electrical cases as serious reflections upon our morality and our integrity as free people. These men were not hoodlums or gangsters. They were highly respected in their communities. Yet they got together in secret, in a classic conspiracy, to cheat their own government: the Army, the Navy, the Air Force, the Department of the Interior and the Atomic Energy Commission, as well as their local governments.

If there is any confusion as to technical interpretations of the antitrust laws, it hardly applies to the area of price-fixing. However, the sad truth is that, although price-fixing conspiracies are the exception rather than the rule, in almost every major community in the country a number of businessmen have conspired or are conspiring to cheat their competition and the public.

One case involved a fixing of prices and rigging of bids in the sale of milk for children in a large public school system. Another involved the sale of bread to the Navy. These are cases that have been brought since the electrical equipment cases.

In almost every instance when we have successfully completed a price-fixing case, competition has been restored, prices to the consumer have dropped, and the competitors who were not involved in the conspiracy have received a new lease on life and could begin to do business again. For example, in a large Western state prosecution by the Department broke up a price-fixing conspiracy among druggists. As a result, there has been a significant drop in the prices which consumers are now paying for prescription drugs in this area.

These are serious cases, in which men who are respected in their communities have conspired consciously to fix prices or rig bids. But I have seen it written and heard it said that they were merely victims of misunderstanding complicated antitrust laws. I disagree. We are talking about clear questions of right and wrong. I view the businessman who engages in such conspiracies in the same light as I regard the racketeer who siphons off money from the public in crooked gambling or the union official who betrays his union members.

A conspiracy to fix prices or rig bids is simply economic racketeering, and the persons involved should be subject to as severe punishment as the courts deem appropriate. When possible, I believe that we should take action, not only against the corporations or companies involved, but against the individuals who have participated in these frauds. I am against granting immunity to the individuals, with the result that the cases end when their companies pay a fine. I think those responsible should be held responsible.

In such cases as price-fixing, or illegal merger or other business techniques for "beating the system," a powerful and vigorous government is not the enemy of the free market. The real enemy is the very businessman who engages in such practices and his colleagues who condone his actions because "business is business." He is the enemy not only because he is stealing, but also because he is destroying the confidence and trust that make a vigorous, free-wheeling economy possible.

Archibald MacLeish once said: "The American journey has not ended. America is never accomplished. America is always still to build; for men, as long as they are truly men, will dream of man's fulfillment."

It is in this spirit, going back to the founding of our

country, that time and time again the American people, facing danger and seemingly insurmountable odds, have mobilized the ingenuity, resourcefulness, strength and bravery to meet the situation and triumph.

In this long and critical struggle, the American system of free enterprise must be our major weapon. We must continue to prove to the world that we can provide a rising standard of living for all men without loss of civil rights or human dignity to any man.

We are going to have to expand; we are going to have to have more jobs and a strong, growing, competitive economy. Our entire defense establishment, including the most secret and sensitive installations, is the best evidence of business and government bringing together the very best talent and ingenuity to keep this country strong, vigorous and prosperous.

Thus I am confident that whatever the problem, whatever the test, we are up to it. But if government, or the present Administration in particular, can be accused of being anti-business, then it might as well be accused also of being anti-Defense Department, anti-State Department, anti-NASA, anticollege, anticlerical and so on. For, unless I have been somewhere way out in left field, we are all working toward the same goals.

CHAPTER 7

Extremism, Left and Right

A century ago Lincoln observed that the dogmas of the quiet past were inadequate to the stormy present. "As our case is new," he said, "so we must think anew and act anew. We must disenthrall ourselves."

Once again, our case is new; and nothing is more urgent than the obligation to disenthrall ourselves from the dogmas of the quiet past. Let us not suppose that we can freeze the United States—or the world—into the mold of today, or of a generation ago.

To say that the future will be different from the present and past may be hopelessly self-evident. I must observe regretfully, however, that in politics it can be heresy. It can be denounced as radicalism or branded as subversion. There are people in every time and every land who want to stop history in its tracks. They fear the future, mistrust the present and invoke the security of a comfortable past which, in fact, never existed. It hardly seems necessary to point out in the United States, of all places, that change, although it involves risks, is the law of life.

66

Nevertheless, there are those, frustrated by a difficult future, who grab out for the security of a nonexistent past. Frustrated by change, they condemn the wisdom, the motives and even the patriotism of those who seek to contend with the realities of the future. They search for the haven of doctrine.

President Kennedy, in the speech he was going to deliver in Dallas on that fateful November 22, wrote that while dissident voices will always be heard in our country, other kinds of voices are being heard in the land today—"voices preaching doctrines," he would have said, "wholly unrelated to reality, wholly unsuited to the sixties, doctrines which apparently assume that words will suffice without weapons, that vituperation is as good as victory and that peace is a sign of weakness. . . .

"We cannot expect that everyone, to use the phrase of a decade ago, will 'talk sense to the American people.' But we can hope that fewer people will listen to nonsense."

President Kennedy felt we deserved better, that as a people and as a country we had the strength, courage and fortitude to face the future. He believed, as he told Congress in January, 1962, that "while no nation has ever faced such a challenge, no nation has ever been so ready to seize the burden and the glory of freedom."

Yet not even in America have all found freedom. Official intolerance ended with the Virginia Bill of Religious Liberty, to be followed by the First Amendment to the Constitution. But private intolerance cannot be put to death so surely.

Religions have for generations been free to preach, to grow and to multiply. If a group of Boston people thought the world was going to end in the mid-nineteenth century, they were free to congregate in a theater, clad in robes, ready to perish together. If Mormons or Christian Scientists, or followers of sects with more limited appeal, like that of the mystic, Madame Blavatsky, have sought to express their faith in new ways, they have been free to do so. If Catholics have chosen to attend mass early Sunday and Jews to observe the Sabbath at sundown Friday, there has been none to forbid them.

But there have always and everywhere been those, throughout our history, and particularly in times of crisis, who have preached intolerance, who have sought to escape reality and responsibility with a slogan or a scapegoat. Religious groups have been the first targets, but they have not been the only ones.

There are those who suspect their neighbors because they pray to a different God, or because they pray to none at all. And there are those who bellow that a former President of the United States is a tool of the Communist conspiracy. There are those who preach that desegregation of the schools will destroy our society. And there are others who believe that calamity will occur because of the way we may treat our drinking water.

There is freedom in this country to be extreme, to propose the most reactionary or the most utopian solutions to all the problems of the country or even the world. There is freedom here to believe and act with passion, whether for the cause of religion or party or personal welfare.

"If there be any among us," Jefferson said, "who would wish to dissolve this Union or to change its Republican form, let them stand undisturbed as monuments of the safety with which error of opinion may be tolerated where reason is left free to combat it."

What is objectionable, what is dangerous, about extremists is not that they are extreme, but that they are intolerant. The evil is not what they say about their cause, but what they say about their opponents.

The intolerant man will not rely on persuasion or on the worth of the idea. He would deny to others the very freedom of opinion or of dissent which he so stridently demands for himself. He cannot trust democracy.

Frustrated by rejection, he condemns the motives, the morals or the patriotism of all who disagree. Whether he is inflamed by politics or religion or drinking water, he still spreads selfish slogans and false fears.

On the so-called left-extreme there is the Communist conspiracy. It is a danger, but it is good to understand just what sort of danger it is because of the unjustified credit of strength attributed to it by the so-called right-extreme.

First, I think that the Communist party as a political organization is of no danger to the United States. It has no following and has been disregarded by the American people for many, many years. It has been studied; attention has been given to it by newspapers, by Congressional committees. And so everybody in the United States has had the opportunity to analyze it. The result is that it is down to a bare minimal following.

Number two, an organization even as small as the Communist party is in the United States (about ten thousand members) is dominated, financed and controlled by a foreign power. In that respect it poses a danger at all times, because it takes instructions and orders from an outside government. The danger exists not in its numbers, not in its political power in the United States, but in the fact, as the Supreme Court has held eight to one, that it is dominated, financed and controlled by the Soviet Union.

Any time that you have a group or an organization in a

country that exists for and takes instructions from an outside and hostile power, that poses a danger.

The Communist party here in the United States has had the vigilant attention of the Federal Bureau of Investigation. That is necessary and that will continue. And the FBI is the organization that can deal with this operation in the best possible fashion. This is not a job for self-appointed patriots or office-seekers working in a hurry or part-time though well-intentioned sleuths.

There is a real sense of frustration in many parts of the United States about Communism, about the Soviet Union. However, in trying to do something directly about it, the efforts, in my judgment, become virtually misdirected. For that reason I think that those who participate in such activities perform a disservice to the United States and to the American people. I think that if these groups and individuals would direct themselves in a positive fashion to positive matters, to making a positive rather than a negative contribution, they could be a help in the offensive against Communism rather than a hindrance.

I have no sympathy with those who are defeatists and who would rather be "Red than dead." Nor do I have sympathy with those who, in the name of fighting Communism, sow seeds of suspicion and distrust by making false or irresponsible charges, not only against their neighbors, but against courageous teachers and public officials and against the foundations of our government: Congress, the Supreme Court and even the Presidency itself. As a vigilant, experienced American who has real credentials as a Communist fighter, J. Edgar Hoover, has said, such actions play into Communist hands and hinder, rather than aid, the fight against Communism.

70

The danger of such views, of the extreme left or right, is not that they will take control of the American Government. In time, the consensus of good sense which characterizes our political system will digest and discard frozen views and impossible programs. But there is a *short-term* danger from such voices. If they cause enough confusion, stir enough irrational fear and attract enough political allies, they can restrict and inhibit a President's freedom to take maximum advantage of the openings which the future may present.

The answer to these voices cannot simply be reason, for they speak irrationally. The answer cannot come merely from government, no matter how conscientious or judicious. The answer must come from within the American democracy. It must come from an informed national consensus which can recognize futile fervor and simple solutions for what they are, and reject them quickly.

Ultimately, America's answer to the intolerant man is diversity, the very diversity which our heritage of religious freedom has inspired.

The largest Scandinavian nation in the world is the United States. The largest Irish nation in the world is the United States. The second largest German nation in the world is the United States. And like statements could be made about other American ethnic groups.

Many voices and many views have combined into an American consensus, and it has been a consensus of good sense. "In the multitude of counselors there is safety," says the Bible, and so it is with American democracy. Tolerance is an expression of trust in that consensus, and each new enlargement of tolerance is an enlargement of democracy.

Part IV

ACHIEVING JUSTICE AND DIGNITY UNDER LAW

"Justice delayed is democracy denied."

CHAPTER 8

To Secure These Rights

> "The law of liberty tends to abolish the reign of
> race over race, of faith over faith, and of class over
> class. [This] is not the realization of a political ideal:
> It is the discharge of a moral obligation."
> —LORD ACTON, 1881

We are today in the midst of a great debate, whether or
not this nation, the champion of freedom throughout the
world, can now extend full freedom to twenty million of our
own citizens who have yet to achieve it. Passage of the Civil
Rights Act does not end the debate. It only shifts the arena
and form of the debate.

Now that we have the Act, one still hears the questions
asked: "Is it needed?" and "Does the national government
have the constitutional power to pursue such goals?"

Clearly, it is needed. No American can condone the injustices under which many American Negroes and other of
our fellow citizens are forced to live, injustices that vary in
kind and in cause from place to place, injustices that are

75

sometimes so intense that in one of our states, with a non-white population of more than one million, of which 442,000 are of voting age, less than 25,000 of those Negroes are registered to vote.

Consider, also, the innumerable difficulties that face a Negro just traveling from state to state in our country, something the rest of us take for granted. If he makes reservations in advance, they may not be honored. If he seeks accommodations along the way, he is likely to be rejected time after time, until, just to obtain lodging and food, he must detour widely from his route; and if he does find accommodations available to him, they are likely to be inferior.

An ironic note here is provided by two of the available tourist guidebooks. One lists only one establishment with overnight accommodations where a Negro can find lodging in Montgomery, Alabama. None is listed for Danville, Virginia. But a dog, provided he is traveling with a white man, is welcome to spend the night in at least five establishments in Montgomery and in four in Danville.

Everywhere we look, we find irrefutable evidence that the Negroes in America have yet to be given full citizenship, and we find increasing evidence, too, that they are no longer willing to tolerate the burdens we have imposed on them.

Many millions of white people, especially in the North—people who until recently assumed that the Negro was satisfied with the great social progress of the past twenty years—are faced now with the startling discovery that it is not true, that whatever progress Negroes have made is inadequate to their need for equality.

And none of us can deny that their need is real, that their frustration is genuine. We have been unreasonable about it, or ignorant of it, far too long. We are only now paying the price. Military and police law have been needed to replace normal local rule in countless cities in the North as well as the South.

This is what happens when long-standing legitimate grievances are not remedied under law. Great moral damage is done to individuals, to communities, to states and to the very fabric of the nation.

We cannot excuse violence from any source or from any group. The responsibility of the Negro leaders who set these demonstrations in motion is very great, as is the responsibility of the white leadership in every community.

But our responsibility as a nation is most plain. We must remove the injustices.

The Civil Rights Act of 1964 is really the first determined effort by the popular branches of government to eliminate second-class citizenship. The "Civil Rights Bill," so long and sorely and famously debated, is now an established fact. It is the law of the land.

The time for eloquence and the supersimplicity of adversary proceedings is over. The time for sober study of our new duties began on July 2, 1964, when President Johnson signed the bill into law. I think that if we learned anything in the Department of Justice over the last four years, it is the heartache, the misery, the pain and the suffering that come from community leaders telling their communities that they do not have to obey the law.*

Obedience will be made easier with understanding. Americans are a remarkable people when it comes to doing what is expected of them. I hope the following lecture (to be distinguished from sermon!) will help to clarify what is expected.

* For more on the general problem of compliance, see below, Chapter 9. —Ed.

77

All titles of the bill are important, but none is of more vital and immediate significance than the public accommodations title (Title II).

For an American man, woman or child to be turned away from a public place for no reason other than the color of his skin is an intolerable insult, an insult that is in no way eased by the bland explanation that it has been allowed to go on for a hundred years or more. It is plainly a wrong and must be corrected.

Moreover, this is the wrong that has caused most of the recent demonstrations. If we can remove this cause, we will be giving the Negroes legal redress, taking the demonstrations off the streets and into the courts, averting the bitterness that will almost surely ensue if we fail.

We may draw some encouragement from actions taken recently by cities in the Southern and Border states to desegregate all or part of their public accommodations on a voluntary basis. But there are many hundreds of communities that have not begun to do so and that will not take action unless there is a law, and unless that law is enforced with vigor.

It has been suggested that somehow a public accommodations statute might interfere improperly with private property rights. However, this is really not a valid argument. Thirty-two states already have laws banning discrimination in business establishments, and most of those laws are far more encompassing and far more stringent than the legislation we have suggested.

Moreover, Federal action in this field involves no novel constitutional concept. Congress often has regulated private business enterprises to remove burdens from the national commerce. The National Labor Relations Act, the Taft-Hartley Act, the Fair Labor Standards Act and the Agricultural Adjustment Act—these are only a few that come readily to mind, and there are countless others.

These old and revered Acts of Congress suggest that Congressional power, therefore national power, to secure civil rights for all is clear beyond question under the commerce clause. And the suggestion that Congress should not exercise the commerce power because there is an overriding moral issue makes no legal or historical sense. It is because of the importance of the moral issue that Congress should act if it has power to act. Child labor, minimum wages, prostitution, gambling—all these raise moral issues, too, and all have been dealt with by Congress under the commerce clause.

There is yet another basis for Federal action, as most citizens have learned in the past year.

Historians have pointed out that the practice of segregation and other forms of public racial discrimination are the product of state legislation during the last quarter of the nineteenth century. Today public segregation and other forms of discrimination depend upon the support of state laws, municipal ordinances and executive and judicial actions. A Federal statute requiring equality of treatment without regard to race, color, religion or national origin is an appropriate means of sweeping away unconstitutional state action and its consequences, and assuring all peoples the equal protection of the laws. For these reasons, the Fourteenth Amendment is also a source of power.

Something must be said of the coverage of Title II, particularly because its opponents have covered it with so much misrepresentation. Title II establishes the right of all the public, without regard to race or color, to the full and equal use of certain places of business which are open to the public. The following types of businesses are covered:

1. Hotels, motels and other places offering lodging to transient guests. Only owner-occupied facilities offering not more than five rooms for rent are excepted.
2. Restaurants, lunch counters, soda fountains and other facilities principally engaged in selling food to be eaten on the premises.
3. Gasoline stations.
4. Theaters, sports arenas and other public places of exhibition or amusement.
5. Establishments which are either located within or contain a business listed above and are intended to serve the patrons of such business.

In case of violation, the victim may sue for a court order to end the discrimination. Primary reliance is placed on state or local laws forbidding discrimination in places of public accommodation, wherever such laws exist. Only if, after a reasonable length of time, local remedies prove futile, may the victim of the discrimination bring a Federal court case. If there are no state or local laws forbidding discrimination, the Federal court is authorized to refer the complaint to the Community Relations Service, the Federal mediation agency established by Title X of the Civil Rights Act of 1964, in order to induce voluntary compliance if at all possible.

The Department of Justice is also granted authority to bring a lawsuit under the title, but it may sue only if the discrimination amounts to a "pattern or practice." As in voting right suits under Title I, provisions are made for expediting such actions, including the use of a three-judge court.

This title does not infringe on private property rights. It does not apply to private facilities or clubs, to private homes or apartments, or, in general, to service or professional facilities. Its aim is to end racial discrimination in public accommodations—in short, to help restore the word "public" to its true meaning.

Title II prohibits any person from denying any person his right to equal service, from intimidating anyone for the purpose of interfering with that right and from punishing any person for exercising such right. However, it is only a refusal to serve based upon grounds of race, color, religion or national origin that is prohibited. A proprietor retains his authority to refuse service to persons who are disorderly, for example, or to decline to provide service for other legitimate reasons.

The other sections of the Act are ways of tunneling in to get at the smoldering origins of the fires of racial discord in our land. Title II takes care of the flames.

Title I deals with the very foundation of our form of government: the right to vote. When we drafted the Civil Rights Bill in 1963, there were at least 193 counties in the United States in which less than 15 percent of the eligible Negroes were registered to vote. In Mississippi alone, this was true in seventy-four of the eighty-two counties. In thirteen Southern counties not a single Negro had been permitted to register. In Leflore County 9,535—or 92.8 percent—of the eligible whites were registered. For Negroes, the figure was 268—1.9 percent. In Tallahatchie County 4,329—84.8 percent—of the whites were registered. For Negroes, the figure was five—less than one-tenth of one percent. There were similar extreme differences elsewhere. In Autauga County, Alabama, 1.5 percent of the eligible Negroes were registered. In Dallas County, Alabama, the figure was 1.6 percent.

We often scoff at the figures cited by the Communist countries showing that 96 or 99 percent of their citizens participate in elections. But what must our attitude be, in a democracy, toward registration figures showing that far less than a majority of the citizens in some states are even eligible to vote?

The Civil Rights Acts of 1957 and 1960 were designed to give the Federal Government legal authority to act against this form of discrimination. Plainly, these statutes have been of great importance. Again, when the Civil Rights debate began in 1963, the Department had filed forty-two suits under these two laws and up to that point had succeeded in obtaining an end to official discriminatory practices in eighteen cases.

In these cases we found shocking instances of discrimination against Negroes. Under the guise of literacy tests or constitutional interpretation tests, barely literate whites have been registered while Negro teachers, graduate students and pharmacists have been rejected for the most technical or imperceptible errors.

Title I reinforces the existing authority of the Federal Government, under the Civil Rights Acts of 1957 and 1960. It does this by forbidding the application of literacy and other tests in such a way as to deny the right to vote to anyone on the basis of his race. To facilitate proof of discrimination in voting cases in the Federal courts, the law establishes a rule of evidence that a person who applies to vote is presumed literate if he has finished six years of school. Of course, local officials remain free to prove that the applicant is, in fact, not literate. The law does not forbid literacy tests; it simply requires that if they are used, they must be in writing.

The standards for eligibility to vote remain the responsibility of the state. The Federal statute neither establishes voting requirements nor controls the states' right to make determinations of eligibility. Basically, all that the new law requires is that state standards be uniformly and fairly applied to all, regardless of their race.

Title I also will expedite the hearing of voting rights cases. Long delays in setting a date for hearings of such cases and the lengthy process of appeals have prevented the actual exercise of the right to vote for months, even years. The new law therefore provides that the more important voting rights cases, involving a pattern or practice of discrimination, may be tried before a three-judge court, whose decision can be appealed immediately to the Supreme Court. It also requires the prompt handling of all cases. Justice delayed is democracy denied.

Titles III and IV are simple, and yet they, too, have not been widely enough understood. A brief look at what we sought to achieve and how we sought to achieve it might help clear up some confusion and ease compliance.

It is well established by many court decisions that the Fourteenth Amendment to the Constitution prohibits racial discrimination in all government facilities—public parks, public libraries and the like, and of course in public schools. Private individuals have brought numerous suits to assert their rights to equal access to such facilities. Many persons, however, are prevented from obtaining their constitutional justice by financial inability to sue or by fear of reprisal.

Title III meets these problems by empowering the Department of Justice, on receipt of a written complaint, to bring suit to desegregate the public facility in question when the complaint is meritorious, when the complainants are unable to maintain appropriate legal proceedings, and when the suit would materially further the orderly desegregation of public facilities.

Title IV deals with one public facility in particular, the public schools. It is now over ten years since the Supreme Court ruled in *Brown* v. *Board of Education* that racially segregated public schools are unconstitutional. Since that time state authorities have been "duty bound to devote every effort toward bringing about the elimination of racial discrimination in the public school system" (*Cooper* v. *Aaron*, 358, U.S. 1, 7). But the record is all too clear that progress toward that goal has been painfully slow.

In 1963 there were still more than two thousand school districts which required white and Negro pupils to attend separate schools. In eleven of our states, with a Negro enrollment of 2.8 million, only 12,800 Negroes, or less than one-half of one percent, were attending desegregated schools. At that time the figures showed that nearly 70 percent of our young white people today had graduated from high school, while only 40 percent of the young Negroes had done so. Of our adult population, twenty-five years of age or more, 22.1 percent of the nonwhite citizens have received less than five years of schooling, compared with only 6.2 percent of the whites.

A state-by-state breakdown of these last figures shows that in Alabama the number of Negro adults who have not completed the fifth grade is 36 percent of the total, while the number of whites is only 9 percent. In Mississippi 39 percent of the Negroes have received less than five years, compared with only 7 percent of the whites. And in Louisiana 40.9 percent of the Negro adults are thus handicapped, compared with 13.5 percent of the whites.

These large numbers of Negroes who were given virtually no education, whom the community denied any real chance of earning a high school diploma, all these people are seriously hampered in their search for employment today.

These are the people whose unskilled jobs are being eliminated by automation, and for whom industrial retraining will be of very little help. The situation can be seen as nothing less than tragic when we realize that the undereducation of Negroes is a clear and direct result of racial oppression—nothing else.

Recent intelligence and aptitude tests clearly indicate that any margin that exists between the scores of white and Negro students is related directly to their social and economic environment.

Education is basic to the future of this nation. When thousands of our citizens are afforded only inferior educational opportunities, they suffer a loss which can never be compensated and the whole country is subjected to unnecessary social and economic waste.

Title IV aids and speeds school desegregation in two ways. First, it provides for financial and technical assistance to schools attempting to carry out desegregation plans.

Second, it authorizes the Attorney General, upon receipt of a written, signed complaint, to sue in Federal court to bring about desegregation, if the students or the parents involved are unable to bring suit themselves, and if the filing of a lawsuit would further the orderly achievement of desegregation. Before taking action, however, the Attorney General must notify the appropriate school authorities and

85

allow them a reasonable time to act voluntarily to adjust the conditions alleged in the complaint.

The law makes it clear that the Federal Government is *not* authorized to deal with "racial imbalance" or to establish racial quotas in schools. No Federal official or court is empowered by this law to issue any order seeking to achieve racial balance in any school by requiring the transportation of pupils from one school to another or from one school district to another.

Title V extends the life of the distinguished Civil Rights Commission for another four-year period and gives the Commission new and useful authority to act as a national clearinghouse for information about denials of equal protection of the laws. The Commission remains without law enforcement powers. However, Title VIII empowers the Commission to direct the Secretary of Commerce to conduct systematic surveys of registration and voting in areas specified by the Commission. The work of the Commission is further supplemented by the Community Relations Service (created by Title X) to help state and local officials and other persons upon their request or upon the Service's own motion. District Courts are to refer public accommodations disputes to the Service.

Titles VI and VII are more economic in nature.

Title VI prevents the anomaly that results when Federal funds are used to support activities and programs that are operated on a discriminatory basis. Racial discrimination in such programs cannot be justified. Equally unjustifiable is discrimination in the employment practices of organizations administering such programs. In short, this title assures the right to equal treatment in the enjoyment of all Federal funds. It is incredible that in our day such assurance is necessary. But such abuses as denying food-surplus supplies to Negroes while giving them to whites have actually occurred and continue to occur. Even so, the Act provides for strict procedures in the termination of Federal aid, and any such termination is subject to Congressional scrutiny and judicial review.

Title VII is the culmination of over twenty years of effort, beginning with President Roosevelt's wartime Executive Order. As long as discrimination in employment does exist, the bipartisan Equal Employment Opportunity Committee will have a vital role to play in securing the blessings of liberty. It is empowered to investigate charges of discrimination and to conciliate disputes arising out of them. Conciliation failing, the aggrieved may bring a civil court action in which the Attorney General is authorized to intervene. These legal actions may result in injunctions against future violations, orders for reinstatement or, in appropriate cases, the payment of back wages.

No criminal penalty is provided for failure by an employer or a union to afford equal employment opportunity. Furthermore, Title VII does not take effect for one year after enactment, and its coverage is limited the first year to firms with more than one hundred employees, the second year to firms with more than seventy-five, and the third year to firms with more than fifty employees. Full coverage is, therefore, delayed for a full three years.

Leaving aside several important but relatively technical sections in the Civil Rights Act, it should be clear to the average citizen what the Act does and does not do, just as it should always be clear to the citizen what his rights are.

This legislation is neither vengeful nor extreme. It is a statement of what should long have been the reality of

America. The rights proclaimed by *Brown* v. *Board of Education* and in countless companion cases must be provided to Negroes at a faster pace, in education, employment and the enjoyment of those things offered to the public. As the Supreme Court pointed out in *Watson* v. *City of Memphis* (1963), these rights are "present rights; they are not merely hopes to some *future* enjoyment of some formalistic constitutional promise. The basic guarantees of our Constitution are warrants for the here and now. . . ." The Court made it clear that the *Brown* decision meant "deliberate speed," not indefinite delay.

By the efforts of 1963-64, in which I am so proud to have played a part, we have gone a long way toward redeeming the pledges upon which this Republic was founded—pledges that all are created equal, that they are endowed equally with unalienable rights and are entitled to equal opportunity in the pursuit of their daily lives.

CHAPTER 9

To Secure These Rights II: A Note on the Lawyers' Crisis

To a far greater extent than most Americans realize, the crisis in civil rights reflects a crisis in the legal profession, in the whole judicial system on which our concept of justice depends.

In this context I would like to discuss three legal propositions. Each of them is part of a time-honored and noble tradition, and yet each of them today is being used to threaten the very foundations of law and order in this country.

The first is the proposition that it is proper and just to avail oneself of every legal defense to test either the validity or the applicability of a rule of law.

The second is that a court decision binds only those persons who are a party to it.

The third is that a court-made rule of law should always be open to re-examination, and is susceptible to being overruled on a subsequent occasion.

All three ideas are basic to our system of justice. But today we have only to pick up a newspaper to see how these honorable principles, used in isolation, invoked in improper contexts, espoused as absolutes and carried to extremes, have placed the sanctity of the law in jeopardy.

Separately and in combination, they are being proclaimed by lawyers and public officials as the justification for tactics to obstruct the enforcement of laws and court orders—as the rationale, that is, for withholding justice and equality from the grasp of millions of our fellow Americans.

We are all familiar with the catch phrases of that rationale, and with the air of righteous indignation in their utterance. The argument goes something like this:

Brown v. *Board of Education* is not the law of the land; it governs only one particular set of facts and is binding only upon the litigants of that case.

Only when each separate school district, each state and each new set of administrative procedures has been tested and judged on its own merits can it be said that a binding decision has been reached.

And furthermore, a decision like *Brown*, repugnant to certain segments of the population and clearly difficult to enforce, may conceivably be overruled as bad law.

To resist it, therefore, is merely to exercise one's constitutional right to seek reversal of a judicial ruling.

When stated that way and surrounded by rhetoric, the argument can be made to have a gloss of respectability. It can even take on the disguise of patriotic, high-minded dissent. Indeed, it is a position publicly espoused today by the governors of two states, by a past president of the American Bar Association and by a Federal District judge who recently overruled the *Brown* decision on grounds that its findings of fact were erroneous.

We cannot blame a layman, even a reasonably fair-minded

layman, for being confused and misled by this kind of reasoning. But to lawyers, it smacks of duplicity. When it comes from the mouths of other lawyers, we must recognize it as professionally irresponsible. And when it comes from the mouths of public officials, we must recognize it as nothing more nor less than demagoguery.

Let us go over those three legal principles one at a time. Let us examine each of them and look for the danger that lies within it.

What do we really mean, as lawyers, when we say that it is proper and constitutional to avail oneself of every legal defense? Surely the Canons of Ethics make clear the impropriety of using dilatory tactics to frustrate the cause of justice. We have only to imagine that principle being constantly applied across the board, in day-to-day litigation, to see that for all its validity it must be met by a counterprinciple, a concept that might be called the principle of good faith. Every lawyer knows, though his clients may not, that nothing but national chaos would result if all lawyers were to object to every interrogatory, resist every *subpoena duces tecum* and every disposition, seek every possible continuance and postponement, frame unresponsive pleadings and resist court orders to a point just short of contempt.

We know that tolerances are built into the system. We know what the margins for evasion and dilatory tactics are. And we also know that the system would be hard put to stand up under a concerted effort to exploit them all. There must obviously be a strong element of good faith, of reciprocity and cooperation, if our court system is to work at all. Take away that good faith, elevate the right to avail oneself of a technicality into an absolute, and you bring the very machinery of law to a standstill.

What about the second proposition—that a court decision

binds only those who are a party to it? Clearly, this, too is a principle that conceals as much as it says.

Every lawyer knows, though his clients may not, the distinction between the holding of a case and its rationale. We know that although the holding contains a specific disposition of a particular fact situation between the litigants, its reasoning enunciates a rule of law that applies not merely to one case but to all similar cases.

Often there is room for much discretion and honest disagreement as to when cases are alike or unlike. But clearly, in the matter of desegregation there can be little or no room for argument in good faith as to when one situation is different, in the legal sense, from another in which the law has been laid down. The county is different; the names of officials are different; but the situation, in all legally significant respects, is identical. There is something less than truth in a lawyer who insists, over ten years after the *Brown* decision and a hundred years after the Emancipation Proclamation, that a law of the land, a guarantee of human dignity and equality, is merely the law of a case. We will have more frequent occasions to ponder this now that cases will arise under the new Civil Rights Statute.

We come now to the third principle—that a court-made rule of law is always open to re-examination and must be viewed as susceptible to being overruled.

No one can prove in strict logic that any given case will never be overruled. But with regard to the position of the court on the constitutionality of the system of segregation, I think we can all agree that the probability of its permanence is so overwhelming as to counsel the abandonment of anyone': hope for the contrary.

No lawyer would advise a private client to contest the valid ity of a position as solidly established and as often reiterated as this one; he would not want to victimize his client by raising frivolous questions. Yet a client is being victimized every time this frivolous question is raised today, and the client is the American public itself.

Right now, all over the nation, the struggle for Negro equality is expressing itself in marches, demonstrations and sit-ins. It seems very clear to me that these people are protesting against something more than the privations and humiliations they have endured for so long.

They are protesting the failure of our legal system to be responsive to the legitimate grievances of our citizens. They are protesting because the very procedures supposed to make the law work justly have been perverted into obstructions that keep it from working at all.

Something must be done, and it is a job that can only be done by members of the legal profession.

First, we have got to make our legal system work. We have got to *make* it responsive to legitimate grievances, and to do this we must work to prevent the unscrupulous exploitation of all the obstructive devices available within the system. Only when our judicial system offers fair and efficient adjudication does it deserve the public confidence; and it seems to me that American lawyers everywhere have a clear obligation to make that confidence justified.

Second, we have a job of education to do. The public must be better informed about the nature of our legal system, and this includes a better understanding of each of the principles and counterprinciples I have discussed, as well as of the legal duties of citizens under the new statute I discussed earlier. Only if we are able to instill that understanding will people with grievances begin to realize that there is a practical and realistic alternative to street demonstrations and sit-ins. But we have to make sure both that there *is* an alternative, and that the nature of that alternative is clearly understood.

If we can accomplish this, I believe we will begin to see a new phase in the movement for civil rights: an increased awareness that direct actions outside the law do not in themselves cure social evils. They serve to awaken the public conscience, and they can form a means of protest when no other means are available. But they will not dictate solutions; they can only alert us to the problems.

And in the long quest for solutions, lawyers have a great deal to offer. We are part of an intricate system that has developed over the centuries as man's best hope for resolving disputes and appraising policies, for working out solutions to problems.

If this system of law, of equal justice for all, can be kept viable, and if people of all backgrounds and of all races and creeds can begin fully to understand and to take advantage of it, then, and only then, will we stand to realize the promise of democracy, both for ourselves and for the world.

CHAPTER 10

On the Injustice in Inequality

> "The law in all its majestic equality forbids the rich as
> well as the poor to sleep under the bridges of Paris."
> —ANATOLE FRANCE

Equality of justice in our courts should never depend upon the defendant's wealth or lack of resources, but in all honesty we must admit that we have failed frequently to avoid such a result.

It was not until March of 1963, with the Supreme Court's decision in *Gideon v. Wainwright,* that the poor man's right to appointed legal counsel was held to be applicable to all courts in the land, at the state as well as the Federal level. I think the story of the *Gideon* case gives us a profound insight into the nature of our judicial system at its best, and into the basic sense of human justice on which it is founded.

If an obscure Florida convict named Clarence Earl Gideon had not sat down in his prison cell with a pencil and paper to write a letter to the Supreme Court, and if the Court had not taken the trouble to look for merit in that one crude petition, among all the bundles of mail it must receive every day, the vast machinery of American law would have gone on functioning undisturbed.

But Gideon did write that letter. The Court did look into his case. He was retried with the help of a competent defense counsel, found not guilty and released from prison after two years of punishment for a crime he did not commit. And the whole course of American legal history has been changed.

I know of few better examples of a democratic principle in action. But in general practice the problem remains: the rich man and the poor man do not receive equal justice in our courts.

Early in 1961 I appointed a committee of distinguished judges, lawyers and teachers under the direction of Professor Francis A. Allen of the University of Chicago Law School to study the problem of poverty and the administration of Federal criminal justice. Within ten days of the Gideon decision we were, therefore, able to prepare a draft bill which has come to be known as the Criminal Justice Act of 1964.

The stated purpose of the Act is "to promote the cause of criminal justice by providing for the representation of defendants who are financially unable to obtain an adequate defense in criminal cases in the courts of the United States." The Act implements in many vital respects the Court's extension of guarantees at all levels in the Gideon case. Now it is up to the bar in every community to see that this Act becomes more than a pay bill for attorneys. It is up to the bar to establish standards insuring that appointed attorneys now will not merely be compensated, but that they will provide competent defense *at every stage of the proceedings.*

But even with the most conscientious execution of the Criminal Justice Act, it cannot, even at best, solve some of the other difficult problems faced by the poor in the courts. One of the plainest of these problems is bail. Its legitimate purpose of insuring that defendants appear for trial has been distorted into systematic injustice. Every year thousands of persons are kept in jail for weeks and even months following arrest. They are not proven guilty. They may be innocent. They may be no more likely to flee than you or I. But they must stay in jail because, bluntly, they cannot afford to pay for their freedom.

Countless cases illustrate the point. Daniel Walker of Glen Cove, New York, was arrested on suspicion of robbery and spent fifty-five days in jail for want of bail. Meanwhile, he lost his job, his car was repossessed, his credit was destroyed, and his wife had to move in with her parents. Later, he was found to be the victim of mistaken identity and released. But it took him four months simply to find another job.

The lesson, in short, is that the present bail system exacts an incalculable human price. And it is an unnecessary price. Repeated recent studies demonstrate that there is little, if any, relationship between appearance at trial and ability to post bail. The pioneering work of the Vera Foundation in New York has disclosed that only 1 percent of persons released on recognizance have failed to appear for trial. This compares with a 3 percent default rate for those out on bail.

I have been deeply concerned about the effect of bail on the poor man. The Allen Committee looked into the question extensively. It recommended that release on recognizance be increased wherever possible at the Federal level, and we have followed that recommendation. In March, 1963, shortly after receiving the Committee's recommendations, I instructed all United States attorneys to recommend that every possible defendant be released without bail. In the first year thereafter, such releases tripled. The default rate, 2.5 percent, is about the same as that for those released on bail.

Even if the default rate were higher, there would still be strong reason to encourage a maximum of pretrial freedom. The studies of the Manhattan Bail Project show the tremendous influence of pretrial freedom on a defendant's eventual acquittal or conviction.

For example, a recent survey of defendants charged with simple assault showed that of those who had been free on bail only 22 percent were found guilty, while 71 percent of those who had to remain in jail were convicted. Again, in petit larceny cases 51 percent of those at liberty before trial were convicted, while 83 percent of those behind bars were convicted. In unlawful entry cases the same pattern showed 23 percent convictions of those at liberty and 75 percent convictions of those in jail.

In a recent opinion of the Court of Appeals for the District of Columbia Judge Skelly Wright had this to observe of the bail system: "The effect of such a system is that . . . professional bondsmen hold the keys to the jail in their pockets. . . . [T]he bad risks, in the bondsmen's judgment, and the ones who are unable to pay the bondsmen's fees, remain in jail. The court and the commissioner are relegated the relatively unimportant chore of fixing the amount of bail."

All these problems, such as competent representation and an unjust bail system, require the wholehearted involvement of the legal profession, starting with law students and reaching to the topmost ranks of our largest law firms. As we see ourselves as leaders in the arena of public affairs, as officers of our courts and as agents of justice, so it is our clear responsibility to work for solutions to these problems, and the larger problems which underlie them.

But it is not the job of the private attorney and the bar associations alone. In George Orwell's world of the future, the Ministry of Hate was called the Ministry of Love and the Ministry of War was called the Ministry of Peace. It must be the purpose of government to insure that the Department over which I presided is more than a Department of Prosecution and is, in fact, the Department of Justice.

These continuing and increasing efforts on behalf of the poor defendant are a beginning. But there remains much work, and great work, to be done. These efforts need to be continued systematically. They need to be enlarged in the Federal system. They need to be explained and displayed to local law enforcement authorities. And there are other concepts which need to be explored, such as the use of the summons instead of arrest.

Thus I was pleased as Attorney General to be able to establish a new Office of Criminal Justice in the Department to deal with the whole spectrum of the criminal process, from arrest to rehabilitation. It will deal with social problems that affect the criminal process, such as narcotics or juvenile delinquency or the right of privacy. It is a voice inside the Department and a forum outside the Department. Perhaps above all, it was my hope that this Office of Criminal Justice would be only the first step in dealing with what I believe is one of the most aggravating problems of criminal law: the wide, and widening, gulf between law enforcement officials on the one side and other legal figures concerned with protecting the rights of the individual on the other.

Differences of opinion between schools of thought on the balance of justice are not only helpful, but desirable, for the dialogue can be creative. But there is little creativity in the present dialogue. For years now, the dispassionate figure of blind justice has been treated to a singular debate between the two schools. One side expresses its logic in such phrases as "coddling of criminals" or "knee-jerk sob sisters." Then in ringing rebuttal from the other side come such phrases as "savage police brutality" or "hanging judge."

The heat of this debate might be entrancing if it were not for the urgency of the problems which it obscures. The present problems of the field of criminal law are deep and serious. The application of criminal law to an increasingly concentrated, complicated urban society affects the lives of every citizen. But because the debate has become so emotionally polarized, there is no common ground for communication or understanding.

There are those quick to criticize the police, without even attempting to comprehend their large responsibility and the difficult conditions under which police often must work. And there are dedicated police officials who believe that the courts are letting them down by erecting all kinds of technical hurdles that interfere with law enforcement.

I mean no criticism of prosecutors or professors or policemen or of either side of this debate. But I *do* mean to condemn the emotional obstacles all of us have allowed to develop, obstacles which block intelligent, and perhaps even fruitful, appraisal of the problems. I became familiar with these obstacles soon after becoming Attorney General, in connection with wiretapping. Wiretapping is a subject of deepest concern to me. I do not believe in it. But I also believe we must recognize that there are two sides to the argument.*

In this regard it is interesting to note that when we introduced proposals revising the law on wiretapping I found that

---

* For more on the wiretapping problem, see Chapter 5, "Eradicating Free Enterprise in Organized Crime."—Ed.

many critics had not even bothered to read the bill. I was further interested by the fact that the American Civil Liberties Union strenuously opposed the bill, while the ACLU's own president, former Attorney General Biddle, testified in favor of it.

The new Office of Criminal Justice can serve as a meeting ground for more profitable appraisal of this and other issues, so that each side may better understand the outlook and the practical problems faced by the other. Even if no consensus resulted, better understanding alone is a goal worth seeking.

However, such a task deserves even greater attention. Lack of understanding rests, at least in part, on lack of information. Crime in an industrialized, urban society is a quite different problem from what it was in the simpler, rural society from which many of our legal rules developed. What we have discovered about the injustices of the bail system is an example. Yet too little has been done to collect and evaluate data about the present operation of our criminal laws.

The time has come for another Wickersham Commission, another comprehensive survey designed to study and strengthen enforcement *of* and obedience *to* criminal law all over the country.* The Wickersham Commission report had a marked effect on criminal law for many years. There are similar rewards to be gained from a new effort.

We should also consider formulating a permanent method to achieve these objectives. In the past, research in the field of criminal law has been left to the law schools, universities and foundations. Perhaps no more is needed. But it is very possible that our laws and our society would benefit from a

* George W. Wickersham, who served as Attorney General under President Taft, was appointed in 1929 by President Hoover to head the National Commission on Law Observance and Law Enforcement, informally, the Wickersham Commission. Its very influential report was published in 1931.—Ed.

coordinated approach such as a National Institute of Criminal Justice, patterned after the National Health Institute.

It is my conviction that the large contribution which now must be made to the field of criminal law is to achieve the communication which such organizations may help provide. But they can only help. The form is not the solution. Better understanding and greater communication will not be achieved by an adversary procedure of emotional arguments. The problem will not be solved by annual meetings. The problem will not be solved by an Office of Criminal Justice. Nor will it be solved by a commission or an institute. It can be solved only by the larger institution to which we all belong, the American legal community. The responsibility rests, as it should, on each of us as lawyers.

No generation of lawyers has yet failed its responsibility to the law or to our society. The role of the lawyer in de Tocqueville's time prompted him to say that "I cannot believe that a republic could hope to exist at the present time if the influence of lawyers in public business did not increase in proportion to the power of the people."

Let us today continue to accept that challenge, whether in private practice or public service. Let us see to it that for all our citizens criminal law means criminal justice.

Part V

AMERICA'S PLACE IN THE FIGHT FOR PEACE

*". . . to that day when Caesars render
unto man what is man's."*

CHAPTER 11

Berlin East and West—A Controlled Experiment

The postwar revival of democratic Europe has exerted a magnetic attraction on Communist Europe. On the dark side of the Iron Curtain, despite rigid Communist controls, democratic ideas, democratic techniques, democratic fashions and democratic ideals are stirring. Among its own intellectuals and its own youth, Communism finds itself on the defensive. The flow of influence is now always from West to East, not from East to West; from democracy to Communism, not from Communism to democracy.

Because the flow of influence goes one way, the flow of people goes the other. This surely is the meaning of the Berlin Wall, that ugly mass of concrete, brick and barbed wire which lies across the heart of the city like a medieval instrument of torture. For the people of Berlin, the erection of that Wall was of course an affront and a source of anguish. But I judge from peoples around the world, from my travels throughout the world, that the Berlin Wall is regarded everywhere as a proof of Communist bankruptcy, a symbol of Communist failure.

Herr Ulbricht himself has confessed that it was to stop the flight of people, to lock up his workers in the workers' paradise, that the Wall was built. For the first time in the history of mankind a political system has had to construct a barrier to keep its people in, and the whole world recognizes the desperate meaning of this act.

They wall their people in. We set our people free. Robert Frost once wrote of it in these lines:

". . . Before I build a wall I'd ask to know
What I was walling in or walling out,
And to whom I was like to give offence.
Something there is that doesn't love a wall,
That wants it down!"

What wants this Wall down is the whole free spirit of man.

The statistics on the flight of scholars offer us an idea of what Communism has done to this free spirit. Between 1958 and 1962, a total of 1,606 scholars, mainly teachers in the humanities and sciences at long-established universities and technical institutes in East Germany, left the Eastern Zone and registered in West German reception camps. More than half are members of faculties; 118 of them are full-fledged professors, a number equal to the professorial component of East Germany's third largest university, at Halle. In those four years Halle lost a total of 147 faculty members, more than the current size of its teaching staff. Humboldt University lost 275 members of its staff; Leipzig, 199; and so on down the list. As the chief law officer of the American Government, I was particularly interested to note, too, the flight of many judges and lawyers from East Germany.

The Wall is more than a demonstration of Communist failure in the struggle for men's faith and hope; it is equally a desperate effort to stem the tide of unification in democratic Europe. By attempting to isolate West Berlin, the Communists hope to subtract West Berlin from West Germany and then to separate West Germany from Western Europe; and, by subtracting West Germany from Western Europe, they hope to defeat and wreck the great cooperative instrumentalities of the regathering of democratic strength, the Common Market, OECD and NATO.

It is certain that the Wall will fail as spectacularly in this purpose as it has failed to seal off Communist Europe from the magnetic attraction of democratic Europe.

Ernst Reuter said a dozen years ago, "Here in Berlin all the slogans that rend the air during the East-West struggle take on a real meaning. Here no one needs any professional lectures about democracy, about freedom and all the other nice things that there are in the world. Here one has lived all of that; one lives it every day and every hour."

And while today Berlin is divided, as Germany is divided, by the decision of the Communists, in the end all Berlin and all Germany are one. The United States shares with all Germans the peaceful but persistent purpose that Germans shall one day find themselves reunited. This is the true path toward lowered tensions and to lessened dangers. We shall continue to hope that as policies of repression fail, and as fears of "revenge" prove unfounded, the Soviet Government, in its own true interest, will come to share this purpose and to cooperate in its realization.

But freedom by itself is not enough. "Freedom is a good horse," said Matthew Arnold, "but a horse to ride somewhere." What counts is the use to which men put freedom;

what counts is how liberty becomes the means of opportunity and growth and justice.

Therefore we do not stand fast at Berlin just because we are against Communism. We stand at Berlin because we have a positive and progressive vision of the possibilities of free society; because we see freedom as the instrumentality of social progress and social justice; because Communism itself is but the symptom and the consequence of the fundamental evils, ignorance, disease, hunger and want. Freedom has shown mankind the most effective way to destroy these ancient antagonists.

The free way of life proposes ends, but it does not prescribe means. It assumes that people, and nations, will often think differently, have the full right to do so, and that diversity is the source of progress. It believes that men advance by discussion, by debate, by trial and by error.

It believes that the best ideas come, not from edict and ideology, but from free inquiry and free experiment; and it regards dissent, not as treason to the state, but as the tested mechanism of social progress. And it knows that diverse nations will find diverse roads to the general goal of political independence and economic growth. It regards the free individual as the source of creativity, and believes that it is the role of the state to serve him, and not his role to serve the state.

I went to Berlin twice, once in February, 1962, and again in June, 1964, after thousands of miles of travel through Asia. I saw men and women at work building modern societies so that their people can begin to share in the blessings of science and technology and become full members of the twentieth century. Social progress and social justice, in my judgment, are not something apart from freedom; they are the fulfillment of freedom. The obligation of free men is to use their opportunities to improve the welfare of their fellow human beings. This, at least, has been the tradition of democratic freedom in America.

Every free nation has the capacity to open up its own new frontiers of social welfare and social justice. Communist leaders have sometimes spoken of peaceful competition as to which society serves the people best. That is a competition which free society accepts with relish.

I know of no better controlled experiment for such competition than Germany itself. The people of West Germany and East Germany are culturally and ethnically the same. There are brothers, cousins, parents and children, some living on one side of the line, some on the other. Both parts of Germany were ravaged by war. Both had the same opportunities in peace. But West Germany elected the free system, and East Germany had Communism thrust upon it.

Only a superficial glance is necessary to see how this competition has come out. The contrast in progress speaks for itself. West Berlin has met the challenge of rehabilitation and the rebirth of justice and of freedom; East Berlin has not. In this city lies an answer to the question of competition. It is an answer so overpowering that it has had to be shut from sight by concrete and barbed wire, tanks and machine guns, dogs and guards. The competition has resulted in so disastrous a defeat for Communism that the Communists felt they had no alternative but the Wall.

And as time passes, the people of West Berlin have become increasingly confident of the future. I saw it in their faces. When we visited Berlin in February, 1962, it was a time of strain and crisis. Men and women cried and greeted us—as representatives of the United States—with expressions that implored us not to let them down. When we returned in June, 1964, a year after President Kennedy's memorable visit, we were welcomed with smiles and cheers and unruffled looks, which we are accustomed to see in other parts of Europe or even in the United States, but hardly expect to find on the front line of the Cold War. President Kennedy's visit was an important symbol for the West Berliners and gave them the confidence they needed. Of course it was more than just his visit that counted. It was our resolution to risk war if necessary to defend freedom in Berlin and South Vietnam and to force the Russians to back down during the Cuban missile crisis plus the evidence on all sides that a free society serves its people best.

We find the same answer all over the world. Few countries were as devastated by the war as was Japan. She alone suffered from nuclear attack. Her great industrial cities, Tokyo and Osaka, were in ruins when she surrendered. No comparable city in China endured comparable destruction. Peking, Shanghai, Canton, Hankow—all were left substantially intact.

Yet today Japan, as I have had the privilege of seeing for myself, has a thriving economy. Her standard of living is higher than that of any nation in the Far East. Her ships roam the far seas, and her airliners fly from Tokyo to New York and London. Communist China, on the other hand, suffers her n^{th} year of hunger. The tragic "commune" experiment has collapsed. Industrial production has slowed down. Poverty and disease stalk the land. Even worse, thousands of innocent people have been imprisoned and killed, and the more fortunate have fled to other lands, more than a million to Hong Kong alone.

Communism everywhere has paid the price of rigidity and dogmatism. Freedom has the strength of compassion and flexibility. It has, above all, the strength of intellectual honesty. We do not claim to know all the answers; we make no pretense of infallibility. And we know this to be a sign, not of weakness, but of power.

The proof of the power of freedom lies in the fact that Communism has always flinched from competition in the field where it counts most, the competition of ideas. The flight of scholars and jurists from East Germany shows the fate of intellectual freedom under Communism. To this day, nearly half a century after the Russian Revolution, one virtually never sees on a Moscow newsstand any book, magazine or newspaper exported from a democracy except Communist party publications. Yet one is free in Washington and London and Paris to buy all the copies of *Pravda* and *Izvestia* one wants.

When will the Communists be confident enough of their ideas to expose them to the competition of democratic ideas? As recently as two years ago a Russian leader, while saying that coexistence with democratic social systems was possible, asserted emphatically that coexistence with democratic ideas was "impossible and unthinkable." It would amount, he said, to Communist ideological disarmament.

I would have thought that he might have more faith in the capacity of Communist ideas to survive such competition. But he may well be right in fearing to let Communism stand on its own in a free forum.

For many years we have steadily sought new ways and means of increasing the exchange of ideas with the Soviet Union. We proudly press the challenge: let the ideas of freedom have the same circulation in Communist states that Communist ideas have in free states. We can have formal peace without such reciprocal competition in the realm of ideas; but until we have full freedom of intellectual exchange, I see no prospect of a genuine and final relaxation of world tension.

For a long time some people have supposed that freedom was the enemy of social and intellectual welfare. A century ago Karl Marx condemned the free economy as cold and heartless, as primarily a mechanism for the degradation of the intellectuals and the exploitation of the workers.

Marx also said that in borrowing the dialectic he had stood Hegel on his head. In the century since the *Communist Manifesto*, history has stood Marx on *his* head. For the free state, contrary to Marx's predictions, has proven its ability to raise mass living standards, even out the distribution of wealth, organize social compassion, advance intellectual endeavor and produce an ever more equalitarian society. Marx's condemnation of the heartless laissez-faire capitalism of the early nineteenth century now, by an irony of history, applies with fantastic precision to twentieth-century Communism.

It is Communism, not free society, which is dominated by what the Yugoslav Communist Milovan Djilas has called the New Class—the class of party bosses and bureaucrats, who acquire not only privileges but an exemption from criticism which would be unimaginable in democratic society. Far from being a classless society, Communism is governed by an elite as steadfast in its determination to maintain its prerogatives as any oligarchy known to history.

And it is Communism, not free society, which has become the favorite twentieth-century means of disciplining the masses, repressing consumption and denying the workers the full produce of their labor. In China today, for example, the state takes away nearly one-third of the agricultural output from the peasant through heavy taxation and compulsory grain purchases below market prices. Far from being a workers' paradise, Communism has become the most effective system ever devised for exploitation of the working class. By this historical paradox, it is free society, and not Communism, which seems most likely to realize Marx's old hope of the emancipation of man and the achievement of an age of universal abundance.

If freedom makes social progress possible, so social progress strengthens and enlarges freedom. The two are inseparable partners in the great adventure of humanity; they are the sources of the world-wide revolutionary movement of our epoch. This movement did not begin in the twentieth century. It began over two thousand years ago in Greece and in Judea. I like to believe that it took its modern form in 1776 in the American colonies.

In some parts of the world today the Communists seek to capture that revolution. But it is always stronger than those who would subvert and betray it. It is stronger in arms, and in the determination, if necessary, to use them. And it is stronger because it expresses the deepest instincts of man.

Berlin stands for the superiority of freedom over systematic suppression. The position of the United States on Berlin stands for our determination not to let the system of suppression win either by default or by naked force anywhere on earth—or elsewhere.

We have stood in the past—and we will stand in the future —for the full freedom of the inhabitants of West Berlin and for the continuation of West Berlin's ties with the Federal Republic and the world beyond.

We have stood in the past—and we will stand in the future —for the presence of Allied forces in West Berlin, as long as they are necessary and as long as the German people so desire. We will not allow this presence to be diluted or replaced.

We have stood in the past—and we will stand in the future —for uncontrolled access to and from Berlin. We will permit no interference with this access, as we have recently demonstrated with regard to the air corridors.

We have stood in the past—and we will stand in the future —for an active, viable West Berlin. Berlin will not merely exist; it will grow and prosper. The maintenance of the integrity of West Berlin threatens no legitimate interests of the Soviet Union, and in due course this problem can be resolved through the processes of peaceful negotiation.

There is no question about the destiny of West Berlin. It will neither be snatched from the tree nor will it wither on the vine. And when historians consider the significance of the Berlin crises of the mid-twentieth century, I do not believe that they will record them as an incident in the encirclement of freedom. The true view, in my judgment, will be to see them rather as a major episode in the recession of Communism.

CHAPTER 12

Achieving Equity in Immigration

It is my conviction that there are few areas in our law
which more urgently demand reform than our present unfair
system of choosing the immigrants we will allow to enter the
United States. It is a source of embarrassment to us around
the world. It is a source of anguish to many of our own
citizens with relatives abroad. It is a source of loss to the
economic and creative strength of our nation as a whole.

President Kennedy took a special interest in immigration
matters throughout his public life. In July of 1963 he submitted to Congress a bill proposing the most far-reaching
reforms in immigration law since the passage of the basic
Act in 1924. At that time he said:

> The enactment of this legislation will not resolve all of our
> important problems in the field of immigration law. It will, how-
> ever, provide a sound basis upon which we can build in develop-
> ing an immigration law that serves the national interest and
> reflects in every detail the principles of equality and human
> dignity to which our nation subscribes.

President Johnson shares deeply in this concern. He gave his emphatic support to the reforms proposed by this bill in his State of the Union Message. Since then, he has several times declared the Kennedy bill to be one of the most significant measures now before Congress.

The whole question of the immigrant and America's historic place in immigration is opened up anew in this bill. It is simple. It is fair. And, when its provisions are understood, it is uncontroversial. The most remarkable thing is that we did not insist on these reforms long ago:

This measure would make it easier to bring to the United States persons with special skills and attainments that we need and want.

It would reunite thousands of our citizens with members of their families from whom they are now needlessly separated.

It would remove from our law a discriminatory system of selecting immigrants that is a standing affront to millions of our citizens and our friends abroad.

It would provide for the needs of refugees and serve our traditional policy of aiding those made homeless by catastrophe or oppression.

And, finally, it would accomplish all these necessary goals without damaging the interests of any person or group, either here or abroad.

Background

The central fact with which our immigration policy must deal is that there are far more people who would like to come to the United States than we can accept.

116

At the present time there are approximately three-quarters of a million people who have applied for admission to our country. Over the next five years another three-quarters of a million will apply. There are differing views of how many immigrants the United States can absorb. But none of us, I am sure, believes we can admit them all.

Therefore the question is not whether quota immigration should be substantially increased, but simply how we are to choose those who are admitted.

Since 1924 our standard for choice has been the national-origins quota system. Under this system quotas are assigned to each country on the basis of the national origins of the population of the United States in 1920. The goal was to preserve the racial and ethnic composition of the population of the United States as it was then.

There are a great many objections to this system. A simple one is that it does not work, even on its own terms.

One reason is that this system assumes each country will fully use its quota. But not all countries do so. England and Ireland, for example, are assigned 83,000 numbers—over half our immigration total—and yet these countries send only about 32,000 immigrants each year. The unused numbers are lost. At present, if quota numbers assigned to one country are not used by that country, there is no provision for their transfer to other countries. Consequently, more than a third of the authorized quota goes unused each year, even though thousands of otherwise eligible immigrants in other countries are eager to be admitted. The failure of the national-origins system is also shown by the continual changes special legislation has made on the pattern of immigration over the years. That pattern so poorly reflects the needs of our own citizens and of our foreign policy that inevitable pressures build up and must be relieved by humanitarian special bills. As a consequence, our actual immigration over the past fifteen or twenty years has been further altered from that purportedly imposed by our permanent immigration law.

A second major objection to the national-origins quota system is that it fails to serve the national interest. No matter how skilled or badly needed a man may be, if he was born in the "wrong" country he must wait to come here, while others who are less qualified come at will. An Italian scientist, or a skilled Portuguese workman, or a Greek chef, or a Polish craftsman with special skills obviously brings more to this country than an unskilled laborer who happens to come from a Northern European country. But now the unskilled immigrant, even without relatives here and with no claim on this country, comes first. There is no good reason for this result.

The third objection to the present system is perhaps even more compelling. This objection is that the system is cruel. One of the primary purposes of civilization, and certainly its primary strength, is the guarantee that family life can flourish in unity, peace and order. But the current system separates families coldly and arbitrarily. It keeps parents from children and brothers from sisters for years and even decades. Thus it fails to recognize simple humanity. It fails to recognize the legitimate interests of large numbers of American citizens.

The Immigration and Naturalization Service files are full of cases which, out of the simplest compassion, ought never to have been allowed to occur. Let me cite a single example.

A Providence, Rhode Island, man, now an American citizen, is seeking to bring his daughter here from Italy, following the death of her husband. Because the father is a citizen, the daughter is eligible for a visa in the second preference category of the Italian quota. Her father's petition for her is near approval, and she will soon be eligible to come to the United States. But things are not so simple, and she will soon be forced to make a cruel choice. While *she* will be able to come to the United States, her three children, aged nine, seven and one, will not be eligible to come with her. Under the regulations, the preferential status that covers the Providence man's children does not extend to his grandchildren. They would have to wait nearly four years to be admitted.

What kind of answer is this for a potential American from a land whose Amerigo Vespucci gave our country its very name? What kind of fairness does this reflect for generations of Americans who came here from Italy in the spirit expressed by Americans like Philip Mazzei, in words later adopted by his friend Thomas Jefferson, that "All men are by nature created free and equal to each other in natural rights"?

What kind of humanity does this demonstrate to our millions of citizens of Italian descent, whose continued contribution to our common country is evidenced simply by a roll call of the Medal of Honor winners, or of political or economic or scientific leaders like Senator John Pastore or A. P. Giannini or Enrico Fermi?

The same can be said about Poles or Greeks or Turks or Ukrainians or Slavs, or of people from all over the world who have given our country its strength. Why should an American citizen who was born in one country be able to get a maid or a gardener overnight from another country, but be forced to wait a year or more to be reunited with his mother— or many years, in the case of a married brother or sister?

The fact is that the existing system provides no reason. Yet it remains the foundation of our immigration law. It simply doesn't make any sense.

Finally, the national-origins system contradicts our basic national philosophy and basic values. It denies recognition to the individual and treats him as part of a mass. It judges men and women, not on the basis of their worth, but on their place of birth, and even, in some cases, on the place of birth of their ancestors.

This system is a standing affront to many Americans and to many countries. It implies what we in the United States know from our own experience is false: that regardless of individual qualifications a man or woman born in Italy or Greece or Poland or Portugal or Czechoslovakia or the Ukraine is not as good as someone born in Ireland or England or Germany or Sweden.

Everywhere else in our national life we have eliminated discrimination based on one's place of birth. Yet this system is still the foundation of our immigration law.

The inadequacies of the system have been deplored by both major parties and by four successive Presidents. President Truman said that its assumptions were opposed to the American tradition and a constant handicap to our foreign policy. President Eisenhower, calling for revision of the immigration laws in 1956, stated that the root of the problem lay in the unfair and discriminatory national-origins system. President Kennedy, in proposing the bill now before Congress, called the existing system arbitrary, without basis in logic or reason.

Now President Johnson, calling for passage of the Administration bill in his State of the Union Message, has urged that we turn away from an irrational and irrelevant concern with the place of an immigrant's birth, and turn instead to a meaningful concern with the contribution the immigrants can make to this society.

Toward Gradual Abolition of the National-Origins System

The bill now before Congress was drafted to accomplish two separate tasks with respect to quota immigration. First, it provides for the gradual elimination of the national-origins system. Second, it establishes a new system for the distribution of quota numbers. Both aspects of the bill are simple in essence, but both involve complexities that need study and explication.

It is clear enough that the present system is unsound and inadequate. However, it is also clear that it cannot be changed overnight. Since 1924 this system has created such monumental inequities that an immediate and complete change would create almost as many problems as it would solve.

For example, there are long waiting lists in Italy and Greece, which now have small quotas. If we went immediately to a first-come, first-served system, without limitation, our entire quota immigration for several years would come almost entirely from those two countries. This would shut off immigration unfairly and abruptly for a number of years from almost every other country.

Accordingly, the bill includes several provisions designed to accomplish a smooth and fair transition from the old system to the new. First, it provides that the old quota system would be abolished gradually, over a five-year period. During each of the five years the old quotas would be diminished 20 percent. The quota numbers taken from the old system each year, together with all unused numbers, would be distributed on a new basis. At the end of five years, all quota immigration would be on the new basis.

Second, the bill would limit the immigration from any one country to 10 percent of the whole number of quota immigrants authorized for the year. Since the total authorized would be 165,000 per year, the bill could not increase immigration from any country to more than 16,500. It seems to me fair and reasonable that no single country, out of the hundred or so in the world, should supply more than 10 percent of our immigration while others waited.

But this limitation would apply only if applicants were, in fact, waiting for admission from other countries. Under this bill, unlike the present law, there would be no unused quota numbers. If they were not used initially by the country to which they were assigned, they would be reassigned to countries which needed and wanted them.

Finally, the bill provides the flexibility needed to deal with unforeseeable problems of fairness and foreign policy. In the past, several of our close allies have established immigration patterns based on our law as it has been. They are not responsible for the fact that the quotas on which they came to rely were the result of a discriminatory system. Sudden change might hurt them unduly. Accordingly, the bill as originally submitted authorizes the President, with the advice of an Immigration Board, to reserve up to 50 percent of the authorized numbers where he finds that it is necessary both in the national security interest and to avoid undue hardship resulting from changes being made by the bill.

The President's authority under this provision would, of course, have to be exercised in strict accordance with the criteria established by the bill, and in no case could the

President give to a country any greater immigration numbers than it has been receiving under existing law. In essence, the President would have authority only to slow the rate at which quota numbers are taken away, primarily from Northern European countries, in the course of transition to a new, fairer system.

As others have tried to explain, the same procedure could be used for the emergency needs of refugees. We cannot know in advance when natural disaster or tyranny will strike. Accordingly, the bill provides that the President may, with the advice of the Immigration Board, reserve a portion of the quota pool for the benefit of refugees.

To insure that these and other Executive functions would be properly performed, the bill would establish a seven-member Immigration Board. Three members would be appointed by the President, two by the President of the Senate and two by the Speaker of the House. Congress would thus be able continually to participate in the administration of the policy established by the bill.

Although the existing system would be replaced only gradually, one form of present discrimination would be abolished immediately. As of now, persons traceable by ancestry to what is called the Asia-Pacific Triangle must come in, if at all, under the quotas assigned to the countries of their ancestors. Thus the members of a family of Japanese ancestry that has lived in Britain for centuries would nevertheless have to come in under the Japanese quota. This provision has little effect except needlessly to insult Asians. It would be abolished by the bill.

The New System

The new system of allocating quota numbers in this bill is based on the system of preferences in existing law. Within the system of preferences, the time of registration would govern—the principle of first-come, first-served.

As under existing law, those who have the greatest ability to contribute to our society would receive first preference. Other preferences, as under existing law, would favor the reuniting of families. If there were two applicants with equal claims, such as two engineers, the earlier registrant would be admitted first. Race and national origin would play no part.

Although the system of preferences used in the bill is based on the preferences in existing law, some changes would be made. Present law grants a first preference only to persons whose skills are "needed urgently" in the United States. Experience has shown that this standard is unnecessarily restrictive. It hinders us from admitting outstanding people who could enrich our economy or our culture. The bill therefore would grant first preference to those whose immigration would be "especially advantageous" to the United States.

In addition, the bill would eliminate the present requirement that to qualify for first preference an immigrant must already have secured employment in the United States. Few businessmen are willing to hire an applicant they have never seen. Thus, as a practical matter, first preference has been available only to those with friends or relatives in the United States who could arrange employment in advance. This requirement has prevented the admission of many outstanding immigrants. Its elimination will serve the national interest.

A further change in the preference structure concerns

parents of citizens and resident aliens. Parents of United States citizens, who receive a second preference under present law, would be given nonquota status by the bill. Parents of aliens admitted for permanent residence now receive no preference at all. They would be granted fourth preference status.

These amendments will not affect large numbers of people. But to those concerned, the benefits will be great.

Finally, the bill grants a partial preference to immigrants capable of filling particular labor shortages in the United States. Under present law, if an immigrant does not meet the rigorous standards of the skilled specialist category, he is not entitled to preference, even though he may answer a definite labor need in the United States which other immigrants do not.

The new system, in summary, is based on the principle of first-come, first-served, within preference categories, subject to limitations designed to prevent excessive benefit or harm to any country. The system is basically simple. It is sound. And it is fair.

There is one item, finally, to which I would especially like to devote a few words. Present law imposes an absolute, un-waivable ban on the immigration of any alien who is mentally retarded or who has, or has ever had, a mental health problem. This provision is a sorry expression of the ancient, discredited view that the mentally afflicted are objects of hopeless shame. It conflicts squarely with the enlightened and humane attitudes toward these problems that Congress accepted when it enacted the Mental Retardation and Mental Health Construction Act.

Our existing law repeatedly creates heart-rending and in-soluble situations. Families which are able and willing to care for an afflicted child or parent are forced to choose between giving up their opportunity to come here or leaving their loved ones behind. This applies also to persons who were once mentally ill. Even though long since successfully treated, they are forever barred.

In many cases these results serve no conceivable interest of the United States. They are in conflict with the medical advances in the fields of mental health and mental retardation.

This bill would, therefore, authorize the admission of mentally afflicted persons for permanent residence so long as the public interest could be adequately protected. The Attorney General and the Surgeon General of the U.S. Public Health Service would be authorized to establish the necessary criteria and controls to protect the public interest. This authority would extend only to close relatives of American citizens or immigrants already admitted for permanent residence. This new provision would foster the preservation of the family unit and eliminate much needless suffering.

These are facts and they are important. But, more than that, I am concerned with the feelings and the fate of thousands of human beings and their families. I am concerned with a very fundamental question which asks whether we believe, as we say we believe, in the dignity and worth of each individual.

The present system is inconsistent with our principles and out of step with our history. This nation was built by immigrants of courage and ability who came from many lands.

I believe that the American people really do not want the present system to continue and that the time has come to enact this bill. It will not solve all the problems of immigration, but it will relieve those which are basic and most pressing. Furthermore, it will demonstrate to the world our dedication to individual freedom and our confidence in the future.

Oscar Handlin, the historian, observed: "Once I thought to write a history of immigrants in America. Then I discovered that immigrants were American history." Let us remember that history and look with confidence to the future, recognizing that our investment in new citizens will be repaid thousands of times over.

CHAPTER 13

Counterinsurgency,
Counterintelligence and
Counteroffensive

We live today in an era of challenge. This is a time of un-
certainty and peril; it is also a time of great opportunity.

The decisions we make as a people, as a government,
during the next few years will affect this planet for generations to come. In fact, what the United States does can very
well determine the more basic question whether there will
even be generations to come.

All of us are most concerned about the kind of America
we want to pass on to our children. Every generation inherits
a world it never made; and, as it does so, it automatically
becomes the trustee of that world for those who come after.
In due course, each generation makes its own accounting to
its children.

When our time comes, we want to make sure that we
bequeath to our descendants a better and safer world than

the one in which we live today, a world in which people will be free from the terrors of war and oppression, free from the handicaps of ignorance and poverty, free to realize their own talents and fulfill their own destinies.

This has been the object of our foreign policy and of our defense policy. It has been our purpose to develop balanced military forces, capable of countering every form of attack, from the nuclear strike to guerrilla warfare, and then use the interval thus gained to work unceasingly toward disarmament and peace. And it must also be our purpose to use every device and means possible to put across our message of progress and hope through freedom. If we won the battle of territory and lost the battle of ideology, we would have gained nothing.

The success of our space program demonstrates over and over again that we are strong and prepared. The fact that millions have watched the launchings demonstrates over and over again that our society is also open and free and that we rely, fully as much as upon our strength, upon this freedom in the continuing hot-and-cold war of present weapons vs. newer weapons, propaganda vs. truth, dictatorship vs. democracy, the state vs. the individual.

I need say little about the character of the Cold War and the Communist threat. The Communist purpose, now as in 1917, is to remake the world in the Communist image. The Communist faith, now as ever, is that history inevitably will sweep all other forms of society, democracy included, into obscurity.

The Communist conviction is that any means is justified to undermine and capture free governments and free peoples. The enormous global struggle which we call the Cold War is being fought at every level. Moscow remains energetic and alert, and its challenge to our freedom is dangerous and enduring. The Communist calendar of ambition is measured in decades, not weeks.

If the free world is to survive, it must above all resist aggression. Aggression today takes a multitude of forms. It requires a variety of responses.

To this end, we have preserved our superiority in nuclear weapons. Our strategic nuclear forces today include 1,700 intercontinental bombers, including 630 B-52s, 55 B-58s and 1,000 B-47s.

We have doubled the number of warheads in our strategic alert forces.

We have increased our Polaris missile procurement by 50 percent.

We have doubled our capability to produce the Minuteman missile.

We have greatly increased our ability to airlift troops and equipment from this country to the point of attack.

Our strength in conventional military forces has been built up from fourteen to nineteen combat-ready Army and Marine divisions.

With the irony of a paradoxical world, the surest guarantee of peace at present is the power to wage war. The United States has that power. It comes from our programs of strength and deterrence. Without this strength we could not have achieved the truly momentous victory of the 1962 Cuban missile crisis. Without this strength we cannot reasonably expect to achieve other objectives even at the conference table in our constant pursuit of peace.

This is not really a controversial point. We are almost all agreed that American nuclear superiority is essential to unanimous nuclear restraint. But as we all know so well, the actual fighting since World War II has not involved nuclear weapons; we all know that aggression is not limited to nuclear attack or even conventional warfare. It was in 1937 that Mao Tse-tung wrote: "The guerrilla campaigns being waged in China today are a page in history that has no precedent. Their influence will be confined not solely to China in her present anti-Japanese struggle, but will be world-wide." That prophecy has proved accurate.

In June of 1962, at West Point, President Kennedy described this new challenge in these words to the graduating class:

This is another type of war, new in its intensity, ancient in its origin—war by guerrillas, subversives, insurgents, assassins; war by ambush instead of combat, by infiltration instead of aggression, seeking victory by eroding and exhausting the enemy instead of engaging him. It is a form of warfare uniquely adapted to what has been strangely called "wars of liberation," to undermine the efforts of new and poor countries to maintain the freedom that they have finally achieved. It preys on economic unrest and ethnic conflicts. It requires in those situations where we must counter it . . . if freedom is to be saved, a wholly new kind of strategy, a wholly different kind of force, and therefore a new and wholly different kind of military training.

We have seen it in Malaya and Greece, the Philippines and Cuba. In Malaya the Communist guerrilla war lasted from 1946 to 1957. It involved 400,000 armed men and caused nearly 16,000 casualties. In Greece the period of conflict was from 1945 to 1950. Three hundred thousand men were involved and 130,000 casualties were inflicted.

We have seen the streets of Caracas become the front line of this era, and Communist guerrillas are fighting today over all of South Vietnam and Laos and in many remote points in the Congo and other African states. The struggle has been broadened today to include violence and terrorist activities that could not even be described as guerrilla warfare. And this really has vastly increased the importance of local police forces and those who preserve an internal defense.

We might well wonder what would have happened in the closing weeks of Venezuela's national election campaign if heroic local police had not regained the upper hand there. And the fate of entire nations hung in the balance during those first turbulent months after independence in the Congo and in Panama and in the mines in Bolivia. These experiences point up the absolute necessity of our maintaining balanced strength. I believe they show that while we seek peaceful settlement of disputes, we need far greater strength in the field of unconventional warfare and the control of violence.

We have made a beginning. We have achieved some notable successes, but we have not mastered the art of counterinsurgency. More importantly, perhaps, in a practical sense, we have not perfected the technique of training foreign nationals to defend themselves against Communist terrorism and guerrilla penetration. This kind of warfare can be long-drawn-out and costly, but if Communism is to be stopped, it is necessary. And we mean to see this job through to the finish.

The substantial increase in our military power, shifting from primary reliance on atomic weapons and massive retaliation to a force which can deal with all forms of aggression, is one fulfillment of the pledge of the United States to meet our commitments around the globe.

More specifically, to deal with Communist guerrilla attacks and Communist-inspired insurgency, the following steps have been taken:

1. A special committee of high officials has been established in Washington to supervise our counterinsurgency efforts on a continuing basis.
2. Through 1964, more than 57,000 government officials, many having high rank and vast experience, will have attended courses dealing with counterinsurgency.
3. The Army special warfare forces are now more than six times their 1961 strength.
4. Special warfare training is now carried out in several languages at the Special Warfare Center at Fort Bragg, the Police Academy and Jungle Warfare Training Center in Panama, and at training centers in Europe, Okinawa and Vietnam.

Out in the field the dreadful battle against the guerrilla continues. Several thousand of our fellow Americans are serving in the undeclared war in South Vietnam. They are there because of a comprehensive program calling for many forms of American aid to reverse the trend in South Vietnam. This includes military assistance to the friendly forces combating the Communists, economic assistance to the villagers who were the Communists' principal target, and administrative and technical assistance to bolster the Vietnam Government.

Having an adequate defense against terrorism is only part of the answer, however. To the extent that guerrilla warfare and terrorism arise from the conditions of a desperate people, we know that they cannot be put down by force alone. The people themselves must have some hope for the future. There must be a realistic basis for faith in some alternative to Communism.

It is for that reason that the United States must continue to expand its efforts to reach the peoples of other nations, particularly young people in the rapidly developing southern continents. Governments may come and go, but in the long run the future will be determined by the needs and aspirations of these young people.

Recall the Hungarian uprising of 1956. Students organized it and led it, and, of course, this movement was ultimately repressed with Russian tanks. But before the Freedom Fighters died and fell on the bloodstained cobblestone streets of Budapest, the world knew them. They had rocked the structure of international Communism to its very foundations. It would never be the same again. Students and young workers rioted in Warsaw that summer with less bloodshed, but with more practical results.

Then came Latin America. Many here reacted in shocked disbelief when the Vice President was jeered and stoned by students in Peru and the windows of his car were smashed by students in Venezuela. Then not long after, student riots in Japan forced President Eisenhower to cancel his visit to that nation and forced the resignation of Premier Kishi.

Two years later 100,000 youthful rioters swarmed through the streets of Seoul and more than a hundred persons lost their lives, but the government of Syngman Rhee was toppled. And the Menderes Government of Turkey fell after violent demonstrations of students and Army cadets. Students played a key role in the overthrow of the Diem Government in South Vietnam as well as the shake-up of the present government.

The Panamanian and American students' actions led to riots in Panama, where more than a score of people lost their lives, and the relationship between our two countries was badly damaged.

These are but a few examples, just in the last ten years, of the impact of youth on the world scene. A number of them, particularly in Africa, are leading their nations. Others are in a position of significant political power. The classroom in many areas is only a few short years away from the Presidential Palace.

There is Kenneth Kaunda, for example. He is thirty-nine years old and has been head of the Rhodesian Nationalist Movement since he was thirty-two. When Northern Rhodesia becomes the independent Republic of Zambia in October, 1964, he will be its first Prime Minister.

Oscar Kambona, Foreign Minister of Tanganyika, is only thirty-two.

Jonas Savimbi, Angolan exile leader, is only thirty.

Sekou Touré, President of Guinea, was only that age when he became President, when Guinea became independent.

Tom Mboya, the Minister of Justice of Kenya, has been in the front rank of his country's leadership for a number of years, and he is still in his thirties, as are Justin Bomboko and Joseph Mobutu of the Congo.

The list could go on and on, and it is not limited to Africa. Rufino Hechanova, Minister of Finance of the Philippines, is thirty-three. Fidel Castro made himself Premier at the age of thirty-two. Nasser and Khanh were thirty-six at the time of their accession.

This is the mark of a revolutionary time, and we should be the first to understand. At thirty-three Jefferson wrote the Declaration of Independence. Alexander Hamilton was but thirty when he wrote his share of the *Federalist Papers*. Madison, who wrote most of the other papers in this great work, was an ancient thirty-six at the time. We were born in revolution, nurtured by struggle and war, over one hundred years before Soviet Communism was heard of.

Over the years, an understanding of what America really stands for is going to count far more than missiles, aircraft carriers and supersonic bombers. The big changes of the future will result from this understanding or lack of it.

We have made some progress in reaching the peoples of other countries. The aid and information programs, the Peace Corps, Presidential trips abroad, all are ways of getting beyond mere government-to-government contact. But the critical moves, the moves that will determine our success, are the kinds of political choices this country makes in picking its friends abroad—and its enemies.

Far too often, for narrow, tactical reasons, this country has associated itself with tyrannical and unpopular regimes that had no following and no future. Over the past twenty years we have paid dearly because of support given to colonial rulers, cruel dictators or ruling cliques void of social purpose. This was one of President Kennedy's gravest concerns. It would be one of his proudest achievements if history records his Administration as an era of political friendships made for the United States. He valued most highly the co-operation established with India, the rallying of democratic leaders in Latin America to the Alliance for Progress, the support won from all the new African states for the American position on the Congo.

It is these examples and others like them now being advanced by President Johnson which will go a long way to determine our future. By achieving harmony with broadly based governments concerned with their own peoples, we do more than make our way easier for a year or two. We create for this country the opening to the future that is so essential.

And to the peoples of those countries we must carry our message with greater fervor than ever. We have the truth on our side, and it would be comforting to think of that as enough. However, as I learned coldly and clearly on my trip around the world, it is not enough. For the truth to be effective, it must be told. And the truth about America, the truth about a free and prosperous democracy, is not well enough known abroad.

While I was in Indonesia, during a question period a young student asked me about the United States, describing its economic system as "monopolistic capitalism." About half the student body laughed and then applauded at this description of the United States, so I called him forward and I said, "Before I answer your question, describe the United States, describe our economic system so that it fits that description." He said nothing. I said, "Well, now, that group of students—" and it was really more than half—"you applauded when he gave this description of the United States. How about any of you coming forward and describing what you understand as monopolistic capitalism in the United States, what it is that fits that description?" And not one of them came forward.

There was a great lesson in this silence. We had not been getting the truth about America to the world, particularly to the young intellectuals in the foreign nations, and particularly in those countries which are just growing, which have just come onto the world scene.

Meanwhile, Communism, armed not with truth but with intensive, attractive propaganda, has been turning them against us.

Just before leaving Indonesia, I met with another group of students and student leaders. There were thirty in this group, and they included about five Communists. They, too, criticized the United States for being imperialistic and believing in colonialism. They dwelt particularly on the fact that we were not coming out strongly against the Dutch in the problem of West New Guinea. They said the Dutch were imperialistic and a colonial power, and the fact that we were not criticizing the Dutch, the fact that we were not critical of the position that they held, showed that we were also a colonial power.

One of them got up and said, "We are against colonialism of any kind. We are against any domination by a foreign country of other peoples." So I said, "Are you against the colonialism of the Soviet Union? Are you against what the Soviet Union did in Hungary? Are you against their position in Poland? Were you against them when they went into Latvia, Lithuania and Estonia?" Then this Communist replied, "Well, those people in Hungary, they wanted the Russian Army to come in. The Communist system is supported by the people in these countries and they have accepted it voluntarily."

I said, "Well, if that's true, why did they have to put the Wall up in Berlin? Not to keep bandits and marauders out, but to keep their own people in." And the answer to that was: "We don't want to get into detail. Let's go back to talk about West New Guinea."

Afterward we had an even more interesting conversation. About six or seven of these young student leaders waited until we had finished packing and were ready to leave. They came up and started talking about the United States. They said that they thought the position that I had taken regarding the Wall in Berlin, regarding Hungary, was completely correct

One of the American reporters, representing the *New York Times*, who was with us asked, "Why didn't you say something at the time? Why didn't you speak out?" The response that the student made was completely disturbing. "We just don't do that in these circles," he said. "We don't speak out when these other student leaders are present. Nobody ever talks out on these matters."

The result is, clearly, that the truth is not getting through at all. In many of these areas it is just not fashionable to speak out for our system of government. This is important, not only for the United States, but for the ideals in which we believe.

How can we respond to such propaganda success, to such intimidation and to such misconceptions about the nature and the motives of the United States? Certainly the devoted efforts of the United States Information Agency and other government and private agencies are having some effect.

But I think, in the final analysis, the truth can only be told in person. And it can, perhaps, best be told, not by officials of one country talking to students of another, but by those with the common bonds of youth and curiosity, exploring each other's countries and each other's minds—in Justice Holmes' phrase, "by free trade in ideas."*

Ultimately, Communism must be defeated by progressive political programs which wipe out the poverty, misery and discontent on which it thrives. For that reason, progressive political programs are the best way to erode the Communist presence in Latin America, to turn back the Communist thrust into Southeast Asia, and to insure the stability of the new African nations and preserve stability in the world.

But however wise our efforts may be in unconventional diplomacy and unconventional warfare, however sensible our diversity of weapons and strategy, however great our military power and determined our counteroffensive of ideas, there is

---

* For an important test case in such free trade, see Chapter 11, "Berlin East and West—A Controlled Experiment."—Ed.

yet another obstacle to our opening to the future. That is the image of the future we project by our own example. What substance can we provide for the international hopes we can kindle?

Thus we end where we began. We must get our own house in order. We must because it is right. We must because it is might.

The following Chronology was prepared on September 15, 1964, at the request of the publisher.

A CHRONOLOGY OF SIGNIFICANT ACTIONS
BY ATTORNEY GENERAL ROBERT F. KENNEDY

JANUARY 20, 1961—SEPTEMBER 3, 1964

1961

JANUARY 22. Moves to coordinate racketeering investigations of all Federal law enforcement agencies. Establishes intelligence unit within the Department of Justice to pool information on nation's top racketeers from Federal, state and local law enforcement units.

FEBRUARY 10. Asks Congress to create seventy-three new Federal judgeships to relieve serious overcrowding in court calendars. The measure was enacted May 19, 1961, and appointment of the new judges began at once.

FEBRUARY 25. Antitrust action commenced in Philadelphia to apply antitrust laws to bank mergers. Department's position ultimately was upheld by the Supreme Court.

APRIL 4. Asks Congress to enact a series of antiracketeering laws to give the FBI and other Federal agencies up-to-date means to combat organized crime, which Mr. Kennedy said had become "too widespread, too well-organized and too rich." Congress, with bipartisan support, enacted seven of these measures in 1961 and 1962, curbing interstate travel and communication in furtherance of racketeering.

Forms committee of distinguished lawyers to study problems of the poor in obtaining justice in Federal criminal cases.

141

APRIL 23. Appointed by President Kennedy, along with General Maxwell Taylor, Admiral Arleigh Burke and Allen Dulles, Director of the CIA, to assess the failure of the Bay of Pigs. The study made clear the nation's need to re-examine and reorient our forces of every kind and led to formation of an interagency committee to combat Communist guerrilla warfare, in which Mr. Kennedy played a key role for the next three and a half years.

MAY 6. In Law Day exercises at the University of Georgia, Mr. Kennedy outlines Administration's civil rights policy, saying: "We are trying to achieve amicable, voluntary solutions without going to court . . . [but] we will enforce the law, in every field of law and every region . . . [and] if the orders of the court are circumvented, the Department of Justice will act."

MAY 20. Four hundred United States marshals are dispatched to Montgomery, Alabama, to protect persons traveling interstate after state and local authorities indicate they either will not or cannot protect "Freedom Riders" testing bus terminal facilities and violence occurs. The presence of the marshals averts mass violence and order is restored.

MAY 22. Members of international narcotics ring indicted in New York City on charges of smuggling more than $150,000,000 worth of heroin into the United States. Ultimately, fifteen defendants were convicted.

MAY 24. Petitions the Interstate Commerce Commission to issue regulations forbidding discrimination in interstate travel, which it subsequently did. This resulted in desegregation of all railway, bus and air terminals.

AUGUST 5-7. Represents United States at ceremonies in the Republic of the Ivory Coast marking its first year of independence from France.

SEPTEMBER 17. Two "Halfway Houses" to keep first offenders from becoming hardened criminals opened in New York and Chicago. These centers and two established later in Los Angeles and Detroit were instituted by Mr. Kennedy to give special guidance to young Federal prisoners about to return to their communities. The centers have cut the return-to-prison rate significantly.

SEPTEMBER 22. Congress enacts Juvenile Delinquency Control Act, providing funds for the President's Committee on Juvenile Delinquency and Youth Crime, headed by Mr. Kennedy, to mobilize Federal resources and stimulate greater local action to prevent delinquency.

DECEMBER 1. The Communist party, U.S.A., indicted for failure to register with the Department as an agent of the Soviet Union. Legal action against officers of the party and some fifty members followed.

1962

FEBRUARY 1-28. Travels around the world on goodwill mission to twelve countries, including Japan, Indonesia, Italy, Germany and the Netherlands, and serves as an American emissary in Indonesian-Dutch territorial dispute.

FEBRUARY 7. The President submits to Congress a bill, drafted by the Justice Department under policy guidelines set forth by the President, establishing the Communications Satellite Corporation—a unique partnership between private industry and the government. The Department played an important role in securing passage of this bill, on August 31, 1962.

MARCH 30. A Federal investigation in Texas results in the arrest of Billie Sol Estes on charges of illegally transporting fraudulent securities. He was later indicted and convicted on this and other Federal charges, and action by the state of Texas also resulted.

MAY 18. James R. Hoffa, general president of the International Brotherhood of Teamsters, indicted in Nashville, Tennessee, on charges of accepting more than a million dollars in illegal pay-offs. This prosecution resulted in a mistrial in December. An investigation was ordered by the trial judge into alleged tampering with the trial jury, and Hoffa was later indicted on jury-fixing charges.

JULY 23. The President sends to Congress a bill, drafted by the Justice Department in consultation with the Department of State, revising the immigration laws. The bill provides for elimination of the discriminatory national-origins quota system, and the apportionment of immigration vacancies on the basis of worth, not place of birth.

AUGUST 28. The Department of Justice files suit in Jackson, Mississippi, asserting that certain provisions of the constitution and laws of the state of Mississippi are unconstitutional because they discriminate against Negro voting-registration applicants. This suit, pending in the Supreme Court, seeks a court order forbidding such discrimination anywhere in the state. It is one of the most important of fifty-nine voting-discrimination suits filed by the Department during Mr. Kennedy's administration.

SEPTEMBER 17. The Department files first of a series of "impact area" school desegregation cases. These were brought against seven school districts which discriminated against the children of Negro servicemen even though they received substantial amounts of Federal assistance to pay for the added costs of educating service children. This first suit was in Prince George County, Virginia, and the court ruled for the government. The Department lost a later suit. The conflict between the decisions is now up to appeals courts to resolve.

SEPTEMBER 30. Following repeated moves by Governor Ross Barnett and other Mississippi authorities to interfere with a Federal court order to admit a Negro, James Meredith, as a student at the University of Mississippi, Meredith is taken on the campus with a force of 550 United States marshals. A night of rioting occurs resulting in two deaths, but the next morning Meredith registers and ultimately graduates.

OCTOBER 14-28. Cuban missile crisis. Mr. Kennedy, as a member of the Executive Committee of the National Security Council, involved closely in the decision-making which forces the Soviet Union to remove its missiles.

NOVEMBER 21. President promulgates Executive Order on Equal Opportunity in Housing, in which the Department of Justice participated extensively.

DECEMBER 16-17. Inspects Inter-American Police Academy in the Canal Zone established by the Counter-Insurgency Committee, en route to Brazil to deliver message for President Kennedy to Brazilian President Goulart in connection with economic crisis facing Brazilian Government.

DECEMBER 24. All 1,113 members of the Cuban Brigade, captured at the Bay of Pigs, returned to Florida, following intensive effort to rescue them from prison. Mr. Kennedy sparked the effort, and the Department of Justice and other government agencies worked around the clock to assist the American Red Cross and representatives of the Cuban Families' Committee. It involved the collection and shipment of $53,000,000 worth of drugs, medicines and similar supplies to Cuba.

1963

JANUARY 17. Argues for the government before the United States Supreme Court in a case involving the constitutionality of Georgia's county-unit system of tabulating votes in primary elections. This case established the principle of "one person, one vote" which underlay the Court's subsequent reapportionment decisions.

MARCH 3. Announces settlement of twenty-one-year-old General Aniline & Film Corporation case providing for a public sale of the company to American interests, and ending government's unnatural role as operator of a private company. The United States will receive approximately two-thirds of the proceeds, providing more than $100,000,000 to compensate Americans who suffered injury or damage at the hands of the Germans or the Japanese in the Second World War.

MAY 2. Amid civil rights demonstrations and rioting in Birmingham, Alabama, President Kennedy sends Assistant Attorney General Burke Marshall there as a mediator. Mr. Marshall succeeds in re-establishing communication between white and Negro leaders. This resulted in an end to disorder and positive later action.

MAY 9. James Hoffa indicted in Tennessee on charges of jury tampering. On March 4, 1964, a federal trial jury in Chattanooga found Hoffa guilty on two counts and he was sentenced to eight years and a $10,000 fine. The case is on appeal.

MAY 22. Begins a series of meetings, soon shifted to the White House, with leaders of business, labor, legal, women's and church groups to seek voluntary desegregation of hotels, restaurants, theaters and similar establishments in more than 70 percent of the cities of the South.

JUNE 4. James Hoffa indicted in Chicago with seven other defendants on charges of fraudulently obtaining more than $20,000,000 in loans from a Teamster pension fund. The trial jury found Hoffa guilty on July 26, 1964, and he was sentenced to five years in prison and a $10,000 fine. This case, like the jury-fixing conviction, is on appeal.

JUNE 5–JULY 14. Participates in discussions at the White House which led to Under Secretary of State Averell Harriman's mission to Moscow to negotiate the Test Ban Treaty. It was signed August 5, ratified by the Senate and went into effect October 10.

JUNE 11. Deputy Attorney General Nicholas deB. Katzenbach sent to Tuscaloosa to oppose Governor George Wallace's efforts to obstruct a Federal court order to admit two Negro students to the University of Alabama. President federalizes Alabama National Guard, and the students are admitted without disorder.

JUNE 19. President sends a new Civil Rights Bill to Congress, the most extensive legislation in this field in ninety years.

JUNE 22. FBI arrests Byron de la Beckwith and turns him over to the Mississippi authorities to be prosecuted for the murder, June 12, of Mississippi civil rights leader Medgar Evers. After two mistrials, Beckwith's case is still pending.

JUNE 26. Mr. Kennedy makes the first of fifteen appearances before Congress to testify on the Civil Rights Bill.

SEPTEMBER 14. Fifteen hundred Negro children, joined by four white classmates, attend school in Prince Edward County, Virginia, for the first time in four years. The President and the Attorney General worked with local authorities and the Free School Association, pending settlement of a long-standing school segregation case.

SEPTEMBER 25. Testifies before Congress on intelligence breakthrough in organized crime. Racketeering convictions under this effort increased from 14 in 1960 to 325 in Mr. Kennedy's last year as Attorney General.

1964

JANUARY 17-30. President Johnson sends Attorney General to Japan, Philippines, Malaysia, Indonesia, Thailand and England as an American emissary in the territorial dispute between Malaysia and Indonesia. Despite a pessimistic outlook, this mission achieved a cease-fire which lasted for six months.

MARCH 16. The Department of Justice, as a central element of a special Presidential task force, drafts the Economic Opportunity Act—the major legal authority for the War on Poverty.

APRIL 7. Eight major steel companies indicted on charges of conspiring to fix prices in the $3,600,000,000 carbon-steel sheet industry, one of the basic subdivisions of the steel industry. This indictment resulted from the price-rise investigation begun in April, 1962.

MAY 29. National Conference on Bail and Criminal Justice opens in Washington under auspices of the Department of Justice and the Vera Foundation of New York, to insure that defendants are not jailed prior to trial solely for lack of funds. In first six months after the conference, more than a score of cities begin bail reform projects.

JUNE 25–JULY 1. Travels to Germany to speak at ceremonies commemorating President Kennedy's memorable trip to Berlin, and continues on to Poland, where Poles greet him with emotional demonstrations of affection for the United States.

JULY 2. President Johnson signs Civil Rights Act of 1964.

AUGUST 10. Establishes a permanent Office of Criminal Justice within the Department of Justice.

AUGUST 20. Criminal Justice Act becomes law, providing that defendants in Federal courts must be provided with paid counsel if they cannot afford it themselves.

THEODORE J. LOWI, the editor of this volume, is Assistant Professor of Government at Cornell University. An Alabamian by birth, he was educated at Michigan State University and Yale. Professor Lowi is a frequent contributor to the scholarly press and an occasional contributor to popular journals of opinion in such fields as urban politics, civil-military relations, political parties, and problems of public policy. He is author of a prize-winning work on New York City, *At the Pleasure of the Mayor: Patronage and Power in New York City, 1898-1958.*

Made in the USA
San Bernardino, CA
11 June 2018